DREAMING
on the
PAGE

TAP INTO YOUR MIDNIGHT MIND
TO SUPERCHARGE YOUR WRITING

Tzivia Gover (signature)

TZIVIA GOVER

THE
collective
BOOK STUDIO

Library of Congress Cataloging-in-
Publication Data available

ISBN: 978-1-68555-012-7
E-book ISBN: 978-1-68555-013-4

Library of Congress Control Number:
2021924393

Manufactured in China

Design by Andrea Kelly
Typesetting by Maureen Forys,
Happenstance Type-O-Rama

10 9 8 7 6 5 4 3 2 1

The Collective Book Studio®
Oakland, California
www.thecollectivebook.studio

Permissions
Lines from "My Cockroach Lover," from
Imagine the Angels of Bread, by Martín
Espada (New York: W.W. Norton &
Company, 1996). Used by permission of
the author.

Lines from "In Praise of My Bed," from
Shubad's Crown, by Meredith Holmes
(Washington, DC: Pond Road Press, 2003).
Used by permission of the author.

Lines from "Henri Rousseau's Bed," by
Charles Simic. Used by permission of the
author.

Lines from the poem "Instructions"
by Edward Vidaurre, published in
JAZzHOUSE (El Paso, TX: Prickly Pear
Publishing, 2019). Used by permission of
the author.

Grateful acknowledgement is made to the
following sources for inclusion of selected
lines:

"The Exaltation of Inanna," from *The
Exaltation of Inanna*, by William W. Hallo
and J. J. A. van Dijk (New Haven, CT: Yale
University Press, 1968).

Lines from "Projector," from *Collected
Poems, 1912–1944*, by H. D. (Hilda Doolittle).
Copyright by the Estate of Hilda Doolittle.

Lines from "The First Dream," from *The Art
of Drowning*, by Billy Collins (Pittsburgh, PA:
University of Pittsburgh Press, 1995).

✦ For Louis, the man of my dreams.

TABLE OF CONTENTS

● PART THREE *183*

It is good to have an
end to journey toward;
but it is the journey that
matters, in the end.

—Ursula K. Le Guin, *The Left Hand of Darkness*

Preface:
Stating the Obvious,
Because Sometimes It Isn't

My idea of an ideal Sunday afternoon is to curl up on the couch with an encyclopedic tome on the science and psychology of dreams—or a book of poetry that makes me feel as though I'm holding someone else's dreams in my hands. That, and the fact that I'm endlessly curious about the worlds inside of other people's minds—which I suspect are universally similar to each other and at the same time stunningly unique—might explain why when I meet people, I immediately want to know about their dreams.

In casual conversation, I skip past small talk and jump to the big questions, such as what a new acquaintance believes is the meaning of life. When I teach an 8:00 a.m. English 101 class, I start by asking my students what they dreamed that night.

When I travel, I'm less interested in the cuisine than I am in what people of various cultures believe about dreams—whether they value or dismiss them, and what they think they mean. I like to ask the woman who sells sarongs in the market in Costa Rica, or the man who is gathering herbs in a small town in Mexico, what their parents or grandparents taught them about dreams. A cab driver in the Bahamas told me she believes dreams issue warnings and premonitions. Back home in one of my poetry classes, a teen mother from Puerto Rico told me when you dream of a fish it means that you, or someone in your family, is pregnant.

Once, when I was taking a water taxi across Lake Atitlán in Guatemala, I asked the driver, a man of about thirty with a radiant smile, what dreams mean to him.

He went silent.

I waited, wondering if the question bored him or offended him, or if maybe he hadn't understood my fast-paced English.

Finally, he explained that he didn't know how to answer my question. Dreams are inextricable from any other part of life, he said. They are woven into the fabric of experience just as thinking is. So, he couldn't articulate a statement about dreams separate from everything else. *Finally*, I thought, *I have met a worldview that matches my own.*

I think of this man now, as I sit to gather my thoughts about dreams and their relationship to writing. I know I should begin this chapter by making a case for why I want to write a book about dreams and writing to begin with, why I use writing prompts that reference dreams whether I'm teaching poetry classes or college writing, or why, for more than a decade, I've been studying the connections between dreams and writing, combing writers' memoirs for hints about their relationship to their dreams, and interviewing writers about how dreams fit into their creative life. But, like the man who drove the water taxi in Guatemala, the connections between dreams and writing are so innate, natural, and intuitive to me that it's hard to know where to begin making my case.

We could start with the bookshelf in your own home. Once you start to look, you'll find that dreams crop up regularly in novels and works of nonfiction alike. They serve to foreshadow events or reveal what a character is feeling before she even knows it. And references to dreams are sprinkled throughout works of poetry as if with a generous shaker of salt.

Another place to begin is when you sit down to write in your journal or at the computer. Maybe it's *because* dreaming and writing are such natural adjuncts that we barely think to comment on or question the connections between them—even while as writers, we instinctually draw on half-remembered fragments from the night as we scratch around for a new idea or an original image. Mostly, we take this storehouse of creative ideas for granted—and barely ever remark on it, let alone give dreams credit, when that credit is clearly due.

But I find great value in stating the obvious—as what's right beneath our nose is all too often overlooked and undervalued.

So, I'll say it here: Dreams serve the writer, and when we write them down, we give new life to the dreams that have been living inside of us—eager to guide and inspire us—all along.

In *Dreaming on the Page*, I'll make these connections explicit. Now, for the first time I am putting these ideas on paper, claiming what I have intuitively known all along: that dreams and writing are perfect bedfellows, and that by honoring both, we can live more fully connected and harmonious lives.

Whatever your genre, and whether you think of yourself as a writer or as someone who is simply curious about their dreams, the essays and prompts, journaling tips, and dreamwork exercises in this book will help you express yourself with greater ease and authenticity. Whether your goal is to finish your novel or to follow your thoughts in your journal to see where they lead, you'll find ideas to support your intentions. You don't even need to remember your nighttime dreams to connect with your prolific, and provocative, midnight muse. The fact is, everybody dreams (whether or not they remember them) and everybody has a story to tell.

So, pick up your pen and get ready to dream.

I am a dreamer, a writer without words. I am a writer, a woman who wants to share her dreams.

—Tzivia Gover, at age twenty-one, personal diary

Introduction:
A Dreamer Without Words
and a Writer Who Dreams

My dreams took up the job of writing coach early on. At twenty-one I wrote in the artists' sketchbook that served as my journal: "My dreams give me advice on writing. They say, *get the idea out first—then leave it for a day and come back.*" That's good advice for any aspiring writer.

In that same journal, sandwiched between outpourings about friendships and descriptions of conversations about art that took place over games of pool, I wrote, "I feel like my life is a novel and I am an English teacher reading too much symbolism into it."

Over the course of a few days, I worked out what has become my ars poetica, an expressive statement of how dreams and writing connect in my life. I typed it up and used it as the epigraph for a staple-bound collection of poems I photocopied and gave to family and friends for holiday presents later that year. It read:

> I am a dreamer, a writer without words.
> I am a writer, a woman who wants to share her dreams.

I spent the next few decades forgetting and then remembering that insight about myself. Again and again, through years when I worked as a journalist at a county newspaper in western Massachusetts, then as the director of a poetry program I created for teen mothers, and eventually as an author and professional dreamworker offering workshops, classes, and individual sessions on dreams and writing, I have flip-flopped between seeing myself primarily as a writer or as a dreamwork professional. But a part of me has accepted and integrated these aspects of myself all along. Starting in my teens, I have kept a continuous record in my journals of my dream journeys and literary aspirations, as well as my challenges and triumphs as a daughter, mother, friend, partner, coworker, and spouse.

This intermingling of dreams into other areas of my life is part of what makes me who I am. My dreams have led me into—and out of—relationships. They've helped me locate places to live, and they've stopped me from moving when I was about to step into a bad real estate deal. They've advised me to stay put in a job when I wanted to leave, then prodded me forward when it was time to go.

My dreams have weighed in on my literary endeavors, too. Sometimes literary role models appear in my dreams to advise or guide me directly: Robert Frost, Stanley Kunitz, and Emily Dickinson have made cameo appearances, for example. (Memorably, Kunitz advised me in a dream to hold any object in my hand that I planned to include in a poem.) A dream might end up in the mind of a fictional character, or it will become the basis for a sonnet.

My journals have become catchalls for dream reports, ideas for books or blog posts, rough drafts, and everything in between. Using one journal gathers all the ingredients into one pot to simmer. Also, recording dreams and waking events in one book affirms the cyclical interconnections between our conscious and unconscious processes—all of which I'll talk more about later in the book.

Articulating these connections for other writers has shown me how important it is to nurture the twin sparks of dreams and writing. For more than ten years now, participants in my workshops and classes have discovered how moving into an intentional relationship with their dreams feeds their writing and deepens the meanings they mine from their dreams.

What You'll Find Here

Foundational to the Dreaming on the Page (DOTP) approach is the belief that dreaming isn't just something that happens at the end of the day, and writing isn't just about putting words on paper when inspiration strikes. Approached mindfully, these humble, holy practices open us to inner dimensions that contain creativity, healing, and meaning. And, like yoga or meditation, Dreaming on the Page consists of simple daily practices whose benefits grow and expand as we circle back to them again and again.

We may not have wings or leaves,
but we humans do have words.
Language is our gift and our responsibility.

—Robin Wall Kimmerer, *Braiding Sweetgrass*

Everybody Dreams . . .
Not Everybody Remembers

No matter how many times I emphasize that Dreaming on the Page is for everyone, whether they remember their dreams or not, there are always those who approach dream recall as if it were a rigid requirement that has the potential to preclude them from participating. This was brought home to me on the first evening of a weekend-long workshop for creative writers who had gathered at a rustic New England retreat center. I had often taught this approach to dreamers, but this was the first time I was offering the DOTP approach to a group who identified as writers but who were new to dreamwork.

I began by launching into my standard instructions for improving dream recall. I reminded them that dream recall is a skill that can be developed, and I introduced them to the basics: "Place a notebook and pencil beside your bed," I said. And I instructed them to repeat their intention to remember their dreams a few times as they drifted off to sleep. Then I told them to jot down dreams or fragments they recalled when they woke up in the morning, or to make some notes if they woke during the night.

There was excited chatter as participants gathered up their notebooks, pens, travel mugs, and tote bags and headed to their rooms in the lodge.

The next morning, when we gathered in our writing circle, I was eager to hear how the night's experiment in dream recall had gone and to introduce the first dream-based writing prompt. Usually after being invited to remember dreams, especially just before bed, participants in my dream workshops tell me their dreams were more prolific, clearer, or more varied than usual. But this time when I asked this group of writers how they slept, I was met with a prickly silence and a lot of uncomfortable shifting around in chairs. Finally, one woman spoke up: "None of us could sleep!" she said.

"Because of you," another woman, steaming coffee in hand, said soberly.

This set off a round of conspiratorial nods and expressions of weary agreement.

Because of *me*? I was disappointed—no, make that devastated. The last thing I want is to rob people of their sleep. After all, I think of myself as the Joanie Appleseed of Dreams. I take pleasure from connecting people with their midnight muse.

"What happened?" I asked.

"The effort of trying to remember dreams kept me awake all night," a woman, who was cocooned in a cozy poncho, explained. And a chorus of nodding heads confirmed the problem.

"I can usually fall back asleep if I wake up in the night, but this time I grabbed my pen, turned on the light, and sat up to write. Then, I couldn't get back to sleep," a young man chimed in.

"And he woke me up, too," his roommate grumbled. "And I was kind of pissed because I wanted to remember at least three dreams to bring to the group this morning."

Despite the desperation in their bleary eyes, I couldn't help but smile. "My instructions last night were meant as a suggestion, not a challenge." Shaking my head, I added, "I've never encountered such a type A group of dreamers before."

We all had a good laugh, then the sleepy writers topped off their coffee mugs to power them through the rest of the day.

Since then, I always remind groups to hold the intention to recall their dreams lightly. And lo and behold, my creative dreamers now sleep more soundly, and most of them recall their dreams, wake in a friendlier mood, and write happily ever after.

And the moral of this story is . . .

. . . Keep a Light Touch

Set an intention to remember your dreams—but don't try too hard. It's better to recall one or two dreams now and then and take the time to really connect with them than it is to grab as many dreamy handfuls as you can, just for the sake of it. Enjoy the dreams that come to you, and enjoy your rest, too!

Here's how to have your sleep and recall dreams, too:

> **Sleep comes first**. Prioritize getting a restful and sweet night of sleep, rather than straining to remember every dream.
> **Dreams are recyclable**. Even if you record only a handful of dreams, that's okay. You can take multiple approaches to working with a single dream, and use it multiple times to inspire new pieces of writing.
> **Minimize disruptions**. Purchase a light-up pen for writing at night, and keep your notebook close at hand (not under the teetering tower of books and tissue boxes stacked beside your bed) so you can easily access both. This will allow you to stay in a dreamy state, and not wake yourself completely, when you want to record a dream in the middle of the night. It will also keep your bed partner or roommate happy, so they can snooze contentedly through your midnight or early-morning note-taking.
> **Just a word or two will do**. When recording a dream in the middle of the night, you don't need to write the entire dream. Often just jotting down an image or a few key words will help you recall the dream in the morning. Either way, an image is worth a thousand words, so it's probably plenty to inspire a poem or story.
> **Too tired to write**. If you wake in the middle of the night with a dream but are too sleepy to pick up your pen, that's okay. Thinking about the dream as you roll back into sleep will help secure it in your memory. Plus, it might help you slip back

into the same dream, maybe even with awareness that you are dreaming *while* you are dreaming (a rich state of consciousness known as lucid dreaming).

In dreams we trust. When dreams are sparse, have faith that they'll return when the time is right. Be patient and keep setting an intention to remember. In time, your dreams will once again knock on the door of your consciousness. So, keep pen and paper handy so you can welcome them in when they do.

Low Recall? No Worries

As happy as I am when I can help a writer remember more dreams, the truth is you don't need to recall your dreams to enjoy the fruits of the DOTP approach. Here are some alternatives:

Many ways to dream. Technically speaking, a dream is a form of thinking (usually in the form of a narrative) that takes place during sleep. In DOTP we expand the standard definition to include daydreams, too.

Dreams have no expiration date. Even people who think they don't remember dreams usually recall at least one dream, whether it be a nightmare from childhood or a memorable dream featuring a lost loved one. You can use any dream or dream fragment for our purposes, whether it was from last night or years ago.

Pick a card. Collect a stash of rich, evocative imagery: Purchase a deck of tarot cards for their vibrant, archetypal images, or clip artsy pictures from magazines, museum brochures, and pamphlets. Then, without looking, pick a card or picture to serve as your dream. Allow the magic of random chance to give you the "dream" you need in that moment.

Waking dreams work, too. When you don't have a dream to work with, you can choose an unusual or surprising event from your waking life to use as if it were a dream. For example, think of a time recently when you encountered an unusual animal, when something broke, or you witnessed an accident. Write the incident down in the first person and without editorial comment. Then work with that "dream report" for the writing exercises in this book.

Reuse, recycle, repurpose. You don't have to remember a lot of dreams to benefit from Dreaming on the Page. In fact, you can use a single dream with a variety of writing prompts and get different results each time. In this way, even a half-dozen dreams can continue to provide new perspectives, precious insights and inspiration for years to come.

Fasten Your Seat Belt, the Journey Is About to Begin

Dreaming on the Page is not a spectator sport. As you turn each page, you will be invited to journal your responses to what you learn, try out new techniques, and implement new habits.

While there is a logical order to the flow of the chapters in this book, there isn't one right way to read it. You may choose to page through it cover to cover, completing the suggested practices as you go. Or you might try out some prompts and exercises in Part Two, for example, before completing Part One. That's okay. Either way, you'll find that when you engage with this process, you will transform dreaming and writing from things that you do into ways that you live.

That said, to make the most of your time with Dreaming on the Page, there are steps you can take to prepare the way for a more fulfilling experience:

Get comfy. Choose or create a quiet, comfortable space where you'll enjoy sitting with your journal for ten to twenty minutes a day to respond to the prompts and exercises.

Set the scene. A dreamy writer's bedside table should be well equipped. Make sure you have a bedside lamp (preferably with a dimmer switch), a sleep mask and earplugs if needed, a notebook, and pen or pencil for writing dreams. (You can transcribe your dreams to your computer or tablet later if you like. But to create the best conditions for sleep and dreams, move anything with a screen out of the bedroom. Or at the very least, keep them out of arm's reach.)

Commit to your bedtime. You don't have to remember your dreams to benefit from the Dreaming on the Page approach, but your experience will be enriched by getting a good night's sleep so, among other things, you can reap the creative harvest of the dreaming mind. Start by committing to a reasonable bedtime *and* wake-up time.

Grab your notebook. Since you've picked up this book, it's likely you already keep a notebook or journal. Pull out the one you are already using or purchase a new one. Start by spending about five minutes before bed reflecting on your day, and another five minutes in the morning writing your dreams.

Buy time. During my workshops, I'm always surprised by how much we write in a short amount of time. It seems like ten minutes in a writing circle is more productive than an hour of writing time alone. I've come to believe in the power of that insistent ticking time pressure. Avoid using your smartphone, smartwatch, or any other connected device for this function, due to their built-in distractions. Instead, use an old-fashioned egg timer or analog watch. Some of my students even use an old-school hourglass. Whatever you choose, set the timer for a little less time than you think you need. (Most exercises in this book can be completed in under twenty minutes.) When the timer sounds, put down your pen and stop. If you're on a roll and want to keep writing, obey the timer anyway. Take a break, stand up and stretch, use the bathroom, or refill your mug if you need to. Then return for another timed session. By doing so, you'll train your subconscious to respond to the gentle pressure of a timed session—and you'll be amazed at how much you accomplish.

Set the mood. Don't try too hard to remember dreams, and *do* pace yourself; you don't need to do all the prompts and exercises at once. Adopt a patient, nonjudgmental, and loving attitude toward yourself as you embark on this journey.

Dreaming on the Page by the Numbers

Everybody dreams, and everybody has a story to tell. These simple facts are at the heart of the Dreaming on the Page approach. What follows is a summary of the principles that have sprung from that basic premise.

The Four Features

Dreaming on the Page is:

1. A unique approach to writing that inspires an awake and aware relationship to creativity by using imagery and information from the subconscious mind, especially nighttime dreams.
2. An alternative lens through which to explore dreams and writing and the many places where they overlap and intersect.
3. A noninterpretive form of dreamwork. Rather than analyze or interpret dreams, we spend time with dreams on the page and allow their insights, fresh perspective, and meaning to reveal themselves to us naturally.
4. A commitment to being an active participant in sleep, dreams, and creativity so we can wake up to lives of increased meaning, purpose, and joy.

The Seven Steps

We often think of sleep and dream recall as things that just happen—or don't—and that are mostly beyond our control. Likewise, we may mistakenly believe that inspiration is a mysterious gift that is bestowed—or not—by some distant muse. The seven steps for DOTP articulate the synergistic connections between sleep, dreams, and writing and awaken us to the power of intentionally cultivating them as follows:

1. **Prepare**. Create conditions for dreams and writing.

2. **Incubate.** Be an active dreamer; request what you need or desire.
3. **Receive.** Open to the dreams and stories/poems that arrive in response.
4. **Reflect.** Engage with the dreams and stories you receive.
5. **Connect.** Be awake to the responsive nature of the universe, including synchronicities.
6. **Manifest.** Take steps to bring the wisdom and creativity from your dreams and imagination into form.
7. **Acknowledge.** Honor the process and express gratitude.

The Five Kinds of DOTP Writing

DOTP writing includes prose (fiction and nonfiction) and poetry in any form that is:

1. **Dictated by dreams.** A direct translation from dream to page with minimal editing.
2. **Filled in by dreams.** A crucial plot point or element is provided by a dream.
3. **Prompted by dreams.** A dream or dream image is used as a writing prompt to catalyze the piece.
4. **Driven by dreams.** Dreams are included in the text to advance the plot, foreshadow future action, provide backstory, expose a character's state of mind, and/or influence a character's actions.
5. **Created with awareness.** Any piece of writing that is created with awareness of the subconscious and/or active engagement with it, despite whether a dream is referenced directly.

The Four Skills

There are no prerequisites needed to begin Dreaming on the Page. But I encourage writers and dreamers to develop these four basic skills to enhance their craft, all of which will be addressed in more depth elsewhere in this book:

1. Dream recall

2. Dream incubation
3. Dream lucidity
4. Active and engaged listening

The Three Basic Tools

1. **Journal/notebook**. A simple spiral-bound notebook is all that's needed for the Dreaming on the Page practice. Computers and electronic devices have their place, too— but are not essential for the DOTP approach.
2. **Pen/pencil**. While there are situations when writing and recording dreams electronically can be helpful, I suggest handwriting for the added benefits that come with the slow and embodied act of writing.
3. **Timer**. To avoid exposing ourselves to the distractions inherent in any "connected" device such as a computer, electronic tablet, or smartphone while writing, use a basic egg timer or analog watch or clock to keep time for your DOTP practice.

Part One

THE SECRET THAT'S BEEN HIDING IN PLAIN SIGHT

Has a writing teacher ever advised you against using dreams in your work? Maybe they warned that dreams are clichéd or a hackneyed shortcut. I've heard that advice and pondered it. But then I remember all the dream-drenched moments in literature that I adore. For example, I admire how Sholem Aleichem, author of *Tevye the Milkman* (the story that inspired *Fiddler on the Roof*), used dreams skillfully in his stories as the deux ex machina—the plot device in which a supernatural force prods the story toward its climax. In one famous example, Tevye uses a manufactured dream to manipulate his wife into breaking off their oldest daughter's match to a wealthy old man, so she could marry her true love, an impoverished tailor. And I have folders stuffed with exquisite poems that feature dreams. Each one is an argument against the scolding teacher in my mind who takes up the party line against dreams in literature.

After all, in a culture where they are otherwise marginalized, dreams show up with notable frequency between the covers of books. Poetry, fiction, and memoir abound with accounts of dreams, and writers regularly attest to the fact that some of their best ideas arose from dreams. Plots may turn on the appearance of a protagonist's dream, and crucial information about characters' inner lives is often communicated through their dreams.

Authors and artists through the ages have known that dreams provide the secret ingredients for producing writing that is captivating and memorable. The poet Octavio Paz cites the example of French poet Saint-Pol-Roux, who would hang the inscription *The poet is working* from his door while he slept. And Jorge Luis Borges said, "Writing is nothing more than a guided dream."

Stephen King found the salient plot twist for *Salem's Lot* in a dream, and Amy Tan has used dreams to help her get unstuck when writing stories. Countless poets from Samuel Taylor

Coleridge to Lucille Clifton have used imagery from dreams in their poems. Literary greats Toni Morrison and Audre Lorde both spoke directly to the importance of being open to dreams and visions in the act of creation. It has even been said that Dante was considered a minor poet until Beatrice appeared to him in a dream. William Styron got the idea for *Sophie's Choice* from a dream, and Sue Grafton used her scary dreams to create her fictional heroine Kinsey Millhone.

Clearly, writing has been a reliable bridge between the conscious terrain of the literate mind and the subconscious realms of the dreaming imagination for as long as people have put pen to paper (or papyrus!) and before.

COLLECT EVIDENCE

Think about all the stories or poems that you love that were enriched by dream content and keep a running list of them in your journal. Reflect on the ways that the dream served the writing. What did the dream allow the author to do better? What can you learn as a writer by studying how dreams are used in your favorite works of literature?

Explore the Storeroom of Your Dreams

When you realize what your dreams have to offer you as a writer, it's like that dream you may have had in which you find a room in your house that you never knew was there. When it comes to the literary imagination, your dreams *are* that secret room. They've been there all along, filled with armoires, shelves, dressers, and closets stuffed full of ideas and inspiration. Knowing how to find this room and access its contents is the key to the Dreaming on the Page approach.

Let's take a quick tour of the riches that you'll find when you look to dreams to enhance your writing.

Vivid imagery. When we enter dreams with our eyes closed, our brain also closes our primary visual cortex (the brain region that lets us see by day). But we see clearly in our dreams thanks to our secondary visual cortex, which wakes up during REM sleep. The result is like turning on the lights inside a midnight museum of wonders and being given permission to return with any object to use on the page when we sit down to write.

Strong emotion. In dreams we can feel intense anger and effervescent joy—along with emotions in every shade of intensity in between. That's because the limbic system (the so-called reptilian brain) is activated in sleep. If you've ever felt like your poetry or prose is flatlining, you can revisit a dream to find an emotional response that fits the scene or stanza you are working on.

A gold mine of metaphor. When we're asleep and dreaming, the parts of the brain that create metaphor light up like the New York City skyline. Our dreaming mind, like our literary imagination, knows the value of comparing one thing to another to make a point—or simply to express what is otherwise ineffable. Think about the motorcycle idling at the curb in last night's dream, and how you woke remembering your youthful passion, independence, and love for adventure. Memories of the summer you spent on the road with your first love flood back as the image lingers, and you sense a need to reawaken that spirit again, even in settled middle age. Study the metaphors in your dreams and use them in your writing, whether directly or to improve your powers of metaphorical language in general.

The symbol store. The tiger prowling your dream kitchen appears with Technicolor verisimilitude, but (thankfully) it is not *literally* in your house. In your waking life that tiger resides within, representing perhaps a part of your instinctual, growling, and fierce nature. Dreams remind us of the power of letting a symbol stand in for paragraphs of explication—and they offer us a dazzling array of symbols to explore in our writing.

Out-of-body experiences. When we read a book, perhaps snuggled beneath an afghan on the living room couch with a steaming cup of tea on a winter evening in New England, we may feel as though we've got our feet in the sand of a distant shore and we might even hear the crashing waves and the sounds of birds screeching as they swoop down to fill their beaks with fish. We're happily hallucinating as our eyes traverse lines on the page of the novel in our hands, just as the author did when she wrote the words we are reading. Likewise, we hallucinate each night in bed with our eyes closed. This fact is so obvious it almost doesn't merit mention, but it does, if we are to map the connections between dreams, reading, and writing. When you sit down to write, remember that, by nature of your dreaming mind, you are an expert in moving in and through imaginary realms.

Animating characters. As writers, we regularly walk around in other people's shoes as we portray a range of personae. We also get plenty of practice in this ordinary bit of literary magic when we dream. Each night you enter a dream body that stands in for the one that is snoozing contentedly beneath the covers in your bed. You might find yourself deep in conversation with an oversized owl in a dream—or you might dream that you *are* the owl. You can bring this same fluidity to the page as you shape-shift in and out of other people's (and creatures') stories.

JOURNALS AND DREAMS: THE UNSUNG HEROES OF LITERATURE

I'm proud of my published books, but I'm also more than a little bit in love with my clutter of notebooks filled with my erratic handwriting and rambling thoughts. Whereas publishing is the equivalent of stepping out with matching socks and my best duds on, journals are where I scuffle about in slippers—completely at home with my hair unwashed. In my journals I glimpse myself as I am: splashes of sweetness, rambling ribbons of confusion, self-righteous anger, pettiness, dull patches of the trivial and the mundane—and brief bursts of brilliance.

Even when I'm embarrassed by the emotions of my younger selves, I'm comforted to find each long-ago me tucked between those covers. Like a kid sister and her too-cool-for-school older sib, we have an uneasy alliance. It's my life's work to forgive and befriend her, to bring her along with me from one volume to the next. It's each writer's life work, perhaps, to gather our lost selves and (someday) welcome them into a wise, wonderful, and singular *I*.

> It is a good idea, then, to keep in touch, and I suppose that keeping in touch is what notebooks are all about.
>
> —Joan Didion, *Slouching Towards Bethlehem*

This intentional relationship with the inner self, the compulsion to understand experience rather than merely living it, and the desire to narrate the journey are hallmarks of a soul who is born to write. And while I know a handful of writers who never journal, most of the published authors I'm acquainted with have some form of notebook practice, and a disproportionate number of them (as compared to the general population) also record their dreams regularly—or at least reliably—over time.

Journals, like dreams, are the unsung heroes of the literary world. Countless works have been inspired by both: dreams and the contents of writers' notebooks. Both are great repositories of raw material for books, poems, movies, plays, songs, blogs, and more. Each of my published books was birthed from the pages of my notebooks and is peppered with snippets of dreams, morsels of dream wisdom, and was guided by dreams.

Not all authors remember or rely on their dreams, but dreamers and journal-keepers are uniquely blessed as writers. We never have to contend with the blank page, because we can use our dreams as texts and lines from our journals as prompts and starters. Like a pot of broth simmering on the stove, the contents of our journals nourish us and provide the basis for countless delicious creations.

But First: A Case Against Journaling Your Dreams

Some days, recording dreams can feel as unnatural as saving nail clippings or strands of hair caught in your comb. Wouldn't it be healthier to rinse dream residue away in the shower each morning rather than gather each one to preserve in notebooks that fill your already-overstuffed closets or basement?

I tend to revisit this question when packing to move, or when I need extra storage space for winter clothes and I'm confronted by the accretion of nearly a half century's worth of journals. That's when I begin to question the conventional wisdom about the importance of writing dreams down, and instead I begin compiling evidence against it:

> **Thing 1.** Dreams don't need writing. Dreams were around long before the relatively recent technology of writing was even developed. So, clearly you don't *need* to write down dreams to reap their benefits.

Thing 2. Dreams resist writing. If you've ever opened a book within a dream, you've probably experienced the frustration of seeing words swim and squirm so you can't make them out.
Thing 3. Statistically speaking, the written word is rare in dreams. (Although writers' dreams are often the exception to that rule.) In this way, at least, it seems dreams and writing don't mix.
Thing 4. Dreams seem to recoil at being preserved on the page; they flicker into consciousness, then dissolve swiftly into forgetfulness. Is stitching them to the page with pen and ink as misguided as trying to sew our shadow to the soles of our feet?

But there's no use arguing, or trying to build a case (or suspense) as to how this question will be decided. Each time I present this argument to myself or others, it is resolved in favor of journaling dreams.

After all, it's not writing dreams down that's the problem. The problem as I see it is this: We're told to *keep* notebooks, but we rarely learn how to *use* them to mine meaning from our dreams or to glean literary gems for our writing. To make our notebooks earn their place on our shelves, we can use them to convert our dreams and musings into poems and stories, and as places where we can reflect on our literary process.

Also, our journals, including the entries that slosh over the shoreline dividing day and night, are central to a way of life that can serve us well. They represent and facilitate our commitment to doing the inner work that allows us to show up more fully for life each day.

Ten *Really* Good Reasons to Write Down Your Dreams

1. **Know thyself**. Journaling dreams helps you better understand yourself from the inside out, which in turn helps you understand your characters better, brings deeper empathy

to your work, and makes you an all-around more interesting writer.

2. **Write regularly—and better**. Building the habit of writing dreams each morning is a great way to build writing into your everyday routine and improve your skills in the process.

3. **A wealth of material**. As you record dreams in your journal, you are creating an encyclopedia of plots, landscapes, characters, themes, and ideas you can return to any time you need material for your poetry and prose.

4. **Build a better relationship**. Writing dreams regularly helps you become acquainted with the Scheherazade within who spins tales while you sleep. Becoming conscious of your nighttime narrator can make you a more confident storyteller and prime you to dream up new material by day, too.

5. **Play with words**. Freud memorably pointed out that dreams are masters of wordplay, including unpredictable puns, clever homonyms and homophones, and layers of meaning hidden just beneath the surface of words. Paying attention to dreams plugs you into these amusing and profound aspects of words that you can celebrate on the page as well.

6. **Magnify the magic**. Tracking dreams can reveal moments of magic (meaningful coincidences, precognition, and clairvoyance—to name a few) in what can otherwise be a writer's relatively staid existence.

7. **Stay calm and moodle on**. *Moodling* is a word that's so much fun to say that I'd love it no matter what it means. As it turns out, *moodling* is a term used by Brenda Ueland, author of *If You Want to Write*, to describe an activity that allows your mind to go slack and dissolve into the present-tense timeless moment. Gardening, doodling, rearranging the figurines on your shelves, listening to music, doing puzzles, and collaging are all ways to moodle. You can also add dream journaling to the list. This seemingly nonproductive time is essential to a productive writing practice.

8. **Too beautiful to hide**. In a letter to his brother, Vincent van Gogh described one reason he painted: "It is so beautiful, I must show you how it looks." With just about anything else we do or witness during the day, others may have seen or overheard it, too. But the dream is ours and ours alone. Writing the dream is how we preserve it so we can learn from it, express it, or share the otherwise ephemeral experience.

9. **A worthy warm-up**. Starting your day with your dream journal and a mug of something delicious to drink is a wonderful way to check in with yourself and warm up to the page, too.

10. **Write your dreams to keep your friends**. When you gush to a friend, "I had the most amazing dream last night!" you may find that most people back up a few paces or suddenly remember an important appointment they need to rush off to. In addition to all of the above benefits of keeping a dream journal for writers, an added benefit is that the page is an eternally patient, listening ear. Tell your dreams to your journal—and save the highlights reel to share (sparingly) with your loved ones.

But regardless of one's philosophical orientation, there is one aspect of dream study upon which scientists, spiritualists, psychologists, and dream therapists agree, and that is the value and importance in keeping a dream journal.

—Barbara Andrews and Mary Michael, as quoted in
Where People Fly and *Water Runs Uphill* by Jeremy Taylor

One Book for All: An Integrated Approach to Journaling

I have tried, with varying levels of success, to write my dreams in a separate notebook, while keeping a second journal where I record my day-to-day struggles, successes, and stories. But eventually, I end up returning to a single, sloshing, ungovernable mass of pages in one book, as my journals seem to insist on their own rules of entropy and cohesion.

And that makes sense to me. Because dreams are informed by our daily activities, and the dreams we wake with each morning affect how we respond to situations in our daily life. Emotions from dreams sometimes cling to our skin. And some days, a memory of a dream seeps into our thoughts with such authority that we wonder whether it actually happened. Keeping one journal for both states of consciousness helps build appreciation for and awareness of this interplay of information gleaned from the day and night.

Or, you can think about combining nighttime dreams and daytime reflections in one place this way: It's like tossing fish skins and potato peelings, apple seeds and avocado pits, crusts and wilting greens into a compost pile. Only in this case we toss in lines from the book we're reading, dream snippets, sketches, goals, pep talks to our discouraged self, and missives to our future selves. The contents stew together for a while, until the pages become fertile ground from which ideas and insight sprout and grow in untamed abundance.

This unified approach also fits the Jungian model of dream-work, in which individuation (meaning the unification of all the parts of oneself) is the Holy Grail of the therapeutic process. In a healthy human, there's a friendly camaraderie between the many selves that are housed within our singular suit of skin and bones. For me, having one journal that holds my Dreamer, Writer, Introvert, Scribbler, Literary Show-Off—and all the other selves within me—is a sign of healthy integration. It can represent a symbolic coming together of the multitudes living within each one of us.

Pick Up a Notebook

Purchasing a new notebook is a great way to mark a new or renewed commitment to your writing practice. But if you are like me, choosing a notebook can be nearly as fraught as choosing a mate, so it's easy to overthink it. Or, maybe for you, choosing a notebook is purely a practical matter. Either way, there are a few things to consider when choosing a notebook and writing implement for your Dreaming on the Page practice.

> **On the page or on the screen.** Before we talk about note-books, let's first consider whether writing on the page even makes sense for your dream reports. Keeping your dream journal electronically (on your laptop, tablet, or journaling app) has pluses and minuses. Studies show that handwriting engages more regions of the brain than typing does—which is a boon for creativity. Then again, when it comes to finding a particular dream, electronic search capabilities can't be beat. I recommend writing most dreams by hand, but typing especially vivid or meaningful ones into the computer, where you can file them and organize them chronologically by month

and year. Experiment with different methods and find what works for you.

Spiral-bound. Any blank book or notebook can serve as your journal, but I recommend one with spiral binding and stiff front and back covers that provide a firm, flat surface for writing when you prop the notebook on your knees in bed. Whatever notebook you choose, it doesn't hurt to select (or create) a lovely one.

Not just any pen. Like many writers, I'm particular about my writing implements (I'm lost without my Pilot P-700 fine-tip pens). But since you'll be doing a fair bit of writing in bed, have some pencils on hand, too. That's because a pencil will write even if it's pointing toward the ceiling while you lie on your back beneath the covers journaling in bed. (Also, it's less likely to stain your sheets, the way pens can.)

A Twenty-One-Day Practice That Might Last a Lifetime

You may be brand new to writing down your dreams, or maybe you've been at it for as long as you could hold a crayon. Either way, let's pause here to consider a structured and sustainable approach to journaling dreams that will enhance your self-growth and literary aspirations. Here's what you'll do:

1. **Commit to the page.** Spend at least five minutes in the morning and five minutes in the evening with your journal. In the morning, write down your dreams. If you don't remember a dream, pick up your notebook and write the words, "In this dream . . ." Sometimes, just taking that moment to consider the possibility of remembering opens the door to a dream memory. If no dreams present themselves, pick up your journal anyway. Record something about that night: how you slept, any disruptions during the night, how you feel upon waking, and so on. In the evening before bed, return to your journal to reflect on the day that

just passed. If you're not sure what to include, use one of these prompts: *If I could preserve one thing from this day, it would be . . .* Or, *Today I'm grateful for . . .*

2. **Mark it off.** Within the pages of our overstuffed journals, we can create enough order to avoid confusion, while still allowing for creative cross-fertilization between dream entries and daytime musings. Draw a crescent moon at the top of the page to mark journal entries that are dream reports. Draw a sun at the top of the page to mark journal entries that are about your waking life. Then, mark the end of your dream report with the initials *EOD* ("End of Dream").

3. **Title it.** Giving your dream a title helps you home in on the most important action, image, or aspect of the dream. Dream titles also help you quickly locate a dream after some time has passed. Over time titles can help you recognize patterns or themes. It can also be fun to title your journal entries about waking life. This is good practice for giving your poems and stories titles as well.

4. **Present tense.** Write your dream report in the present tense, as if it is happening now. This will help you tune into the dream and keep the energy, emotion, and action alive on the page. Try keeping this present-moment awareness with you all day long, too.

5. **Just the dream.** When writing down your dreams, leave aside commentary or associations until later. The objective here is to keep the world of the dream intact. After all, if you were writing a scene from a novel, you wouldn't interrupt the action to write, "The character of Jeremy is based on my high school boyfriend. Except now he has full eyebrows like my boss does, and he's much shorter." Rather, you'd just write, "Jeremy, a short man with full eyebrows, took me in his arms and . . ." Likewise, describe the characters and settings in your dreams as they are.

6. **Details, please.** Include as much sensory detail as you can when writing a dream, including the quality of light,

colors, sounds, and sensations. If you are pressed for time, choose one scene or image to describe in detail and jot down notes on the rest. The more you practice noticing, the more you will notice. This will also help build your powers of observation throughout the day, which will enrich your experience overall. Developing an eye for detail will also serve your writing as you craft poems, stories, and essays.

7. **Emotional territory**. After you write down your dream, record the predominant emotion you experienced. This can be trickier than it sounds. You may recall a dream, but not what you were feeling in it. If so, take a moment and reimagine yourself inside the dream. Breathe. Feel into your body and identify any areas of tension, jittery aliveness, heaviness, and so on. Often the emotion can be found within these visceral sensations. Tuning into emotions in dreams makes us more emotionally literate in our daily lives, too. Also, as writers, this emotional fluency helps us delve deeper into the hearts of our characters.

8. **Review it**. Draw a blank box beside a snippet, poetic line, or story idea that you'd like to revisit later, or that serves a larger project that is currently underway. At intervals (monthly or seasonally) review your journal and lift out pieces you've marked that might serve other projects, such as images from dreams, bits of overheard conversation, a single line from an otherwise flop of a poem, or an idea that might inspire an essay or blog post or be integrated into a larger manuscript. We'll discuss this more in Part Three.

9. **Journal in living color**. Keep a bowl, basket, or pouch filled with colored pencils, highlighters, scissors, and a glue stick nearby when you journal. Add a sketch or collage element to dream reports or descriptions of waking events. This has a practical benefit, as illustrations can help you express what you saw in a dream or your waking life. Like dream titles, drawings can also help you quickly locate a particular

journal entry later on. Plus, adding a dash of color signals to your creative muse that you're ready to play. That's serious business when we remember that play is a source of flexible thinking, out-of-the-box experimentation, and inventive problem-solving—all of which are essential qualities for dreamy writers.

10. **Count the days.** I suggest you follow this format for the next twenty-one days. After that, this journaling habit and method should become second nature. If not, or if after a period of time you lose momentum, you can tweak this process to better suit your needs. For example, you might decide to journal only briefly on weekdays, but to include a longer catch-up session on weekends. You can also restart the twenty-one-day practice anytime to try again to build the habit of regular journaling.

Take Your Dreams into Your Day

Until you picked up this book, you might have thought of sleep as a passive activity, and you may have regarded dreaming as something that just happens *to* you—rather than something you can develop through practice and attention. Likewise, you may have thought of creativity and literary talent as something that you have or you don't. But you can take an active role to recall more dreams, incubate dreams on a particular topic, and bring lucidity to your dreams to recharge your creativity. Writing down your dreams is a powerful way to connect with them and integrate their wisdom into your daily life.

We are all empowered creators of our life stories. So, before you put down your pen and close your dream journal, consider how you might bring your dreams from the pillow to the page, and into your day. When you take a small action in response to your dreams, you help bring their messages into consciousness so you can reap the benefits of your dreaming mind—regardless of whether you fully understand your dreams. For example:

Touch in with something special. An easy and meaningful way to honor your dreams is to connect with something that reminds you of them during the day. For example, if I dream I am eating bright red strawberries, I might buy a pint and think about the dream as I slice and eat the fruit. Or, if I dream I am swimming in a beautiful blue lake, I might take a swim or a bath the next day, and think about the dream as I soak in the water.

Affirm it. Another way to honor your dream is to create a short positive statement in the present tense. For example, an affirmation based on the dream about strawberries might go something like this: "I recognize and enjoy the natural sweetness in my life." Make your affirmation short and direct, like something you might read on a bumper sticker. Keeping it concise and closely connected to the imagery from your dream will help you remember it. You can also copy it onto an index card and post it where you will see it and be inspired by it.

Mine the wisdom. Use these prompts to help you articulate your dream's wisdom and carry it into your day:

> *In order for me to be healthy, whole, and complete, my dream may be suggesting that I _____ .*
> *I will honor my dream today by taking this small step:*
> _____ .

Remember: When it comes to honoring your dreams, less can be more, and a little bit goes a long way. So, keep your affirmations and actions small and simple.

Writing Down the Dream

For writers, one of the most exciting and productive ways to take dreams off the pillow is to put them on the page. You'll receive a plethora of prompts and exercises for doing so in Part Two. But you don't have to wait. Here are a few ways you can get started now:

Make a dreamy draft. Use last night's dream, or any dream you remember, as a first draft of a story or a poem.

Start a sentence. Use a phrase from a dream as a sentence starter to inspire a poem or the next paragraph in a story you are writing.

Follow the script. Write a dream as if it were the script for a movie or a play. Incorporate dialogue, stage directions, cuts, fades, and the like.

First, second, or third. Try writing a dream in the second or third person, switching from the habitual *I* to either *he/she/they* or *you*. Notice how this simple shift in perspective alters the tone and feeling of the dream and opens new literary possibilities.

A (VERY) BRIEF HISTORY OF DREAMS AND WRITING

Reaching back in time through all of human history, we are reminded that mixing dreams and writing is a relatively recent phenomenon. Paleolithic cave art, for example, is thought to have significant dream content—and was created long before anyone picked up a pen, let alone tapped out words on a keyboard. The earliest writing system dates back to Mesopotamia more than 5,500 years ago. As it developed over the next few millennia, writing was a technology relegated to the select few—usually members of the priestly class. It wasn't until the Industrial Revolution in the eighteenth and nineteenth centuries that literacy became a more universally valued competency.

Dreams, meanwhile, have played a pivotal role in the telling of the human story. Going back to the Paleolithic era, writing a story took a lot more effort than tapping out words on a keyboard and rearranging them with the swish of a mouse on a screen. People created pigment from clay, sea shells, soot, and charcoal and painted dream stories onto cave walls. Dreams were featured in the hymns of the first priestess-poet, and in the *Epic of Gilgamesh*, the *Rig-Veda*, the Hebrew Bible, and the Quran, as well as other ancient sacred texts and sagas.

Now let's take a step back in time and look at the long, rich, and interconnected history of dreams and writing.

That which I recited to you at (mid)night
May the singer repeat it to you at noon!

—Enheduanna, "The Exaltation of Inanna"

The Secret (Past) Lives of Dreams and Writing

Genesis, the myth of human origins as recorded in the best-selling book of all time, showcases the power of words to build worlds. In the beginning, God spoke the world into being. Six days later, the world was fully formed.

We don't know on which day of this story dreams appeared, but we can safely say that nighttime narratives predate written language by millennia. After all, in the development of human history, as well as in each individual lifetime, dreams come first. Babies dream in the womb long before they learn to speak, let alone write.

As for the creation of the written word, we don't know the exact date that writing was created, but we can dream into one of the early appearances of the written word, as formed by the hand of the first known poet. Squint your eyes and peer back in time, to a night some four thousand years ago. There you might glimpse a robed priestess named Enheduanna, seated in her chamber, eyes narrowed as she, too, strains to see into other worlds. Bent over in concentration, her wrist rocks back and forth as she presses a reed stylus into a clay tablet and carves wedge-shaped divots into the moist surface. She makes out the letters she is forming through ribbons of smoke rising from the orange coals glowing in an earthenware pot beside her.

Even if we could get close enough, most of us could not decipher the cuneiform characters she is inscribing, and no matter how hard we looked we couldn't see the half-dream that holds her attention. As she works, in the theater of her mind

Enheduanna sees a goddess with a quiver of slender spears fanning out from a harness on her back. The familiar voice of her muse is as real to her as the sounds of animals scuffling outside in the night and the flames snapping against the air within the censer beside her. She pauses to catch each word, then transcribes them, line by line, into the waiting clay.

For contemporary writers, the most compelling descriptions from her surviving poems and hymns to gods and goddesses might be those that reveal her creative process. Like many writers (perhaps you are among them) who say they do their best writing after everyone else has gone to bed or before others wake in the morning, Enheduanna wrote in the darkness of night. She began with a ritual to help her move into a quiet, inner space. She then invited her subject, in this case the goddess Inanna, to speak through her.

While I don't know any writers whose ritual includes burning coals in a censer as Enheduanna did, I know many who light a candle, play entrancing music, or fill a mug with their favorite brew. They may also meditate before they begin to compose.

As for me, before sitting down at the keyboard this morning, I closed my eyes for a few minutes of quiet prayer and reflection, as I do most days. Then I pushed the button on the electric diffuser at the corner of my desk, and rosemary-scented steam rose into the air. From time to time I pause, sip my tea, and close my eyes to let the words from the pages of research piled at my elbow and the thoughts in the domed chamber of my imagination roil about, then settle. I can almost smell the smoke from Enheduanna's censer, as if it is mingling with the scented steam from my diffuser. Then, I return my fingertips to the keys and write.

Like Enheduanna, many of us continue to court the hushed hours when others are sleeping to practice our craft. We revel in the liminal magic that we sense at those times. Like the first poet, we may even have a small ritual to help us prepare to cross the threshold from one realm to the other, from the conscious mind to the subconscious, or from the waking mind to the dreamy imagination.

Historian Roberta Binkley writes: "[Enheduanna's] composing process is one I read as collaborative with the goddess. She and Inanna become one for a while and from the deep collaboration—an inspiriting of in-fusing—she gives birth to the hymn."[1] Writing, then, has always been co-creation: whether between the writer and the characters she dreams up, or with inner voices, whether wise, or funny, or divine. Or, we might channel inspiration from our dreams directly to the page.

Dream Chronology

Now that we've taken a long view of human history, let's consider the span of one life: yours. Remember the timelines you made in history class? Get out your notebook and create a timeline on which you plot life events that relate to you and your relationship to dreams and writing.

1. Hold a piece of paper sideways (landscape orientation) and draw a horizontal line across it.
2. On the far left make a dot and label it with the date of your birth and on the far right make a dot and label it with today's date.
3. In between, plot out points for your first remembered dream; early attempts at writing stories or poems; memories about sleep and nighttime from childhood forward, such as memorable dreams or nightmares. You might also include the first time you shared your writing with others; your first publication; or any other experiences that contributed to how you relate to sleep and dreams or your life as a writer and creative soul.
4. Plot "big-picture" points, too: What social, political, pop culture, or historical events influenced you as a writer or dreamer? Was there a cause that inspired you to write a poem or letter? Was your understanding of sleep or dreams expanded by breakthroughs in psychology or science, such as the first evidence of lucid dreaming? Perhaps there was a song or movie that changed how you value your inner life?

5. Review your timeline. You can look at the entire expanse of time, or break your review into distinct periods (decades or five-year blocks, for example) one at a time. Notice any patterns and try to take in the overall shape as you reflect on the evolving nature of your dreams and writing. When you are done, reflect in your journal: What have you learned about your personal history with dreams and writing?

WRITTEN ON THE BRAIN

Until the advent of writing, stories needed to be transported, one voice at a time. Human memory was required to store each one, and the knowledge and collected wisdom they contained, so they could reach neighboring villages, distant continents, and future generations.

With the invention of writing, odes and epics were no longer at the mercy of diaphragm, throat, tongue, and teeth—and the willing ear of a nearby listener—to survive. Nor did people need to rely solely on memory to preserve them. Storytelling, and civilizations, were forever changed, and so, too, was the human brain.

> **No good poem was ever written which was the product wholly of the poet's conscious mind.**
>
> **—Robert Nye, poet and novelist**

As writing evolved from pictographs carved in stone to abstract marks inked onto paper, the language centers that process the written word grew larger. With the rise of literacy, abstract thought became more highly developed. The regions of the brain that are associated with logic, sequencing, and linear forms of thinking also grew and became more finely tuned. Meanwhile, the right-brain intuitive and creative faculties— which also happen to be characteristics of the dreaming brain, diminished by comparison.

Perhaps it is no coincidence, then, that in our highly literate and technology-obsessed society, nearly all the dreams dreamed (five to seven per person per night worldwide) are forgotten. The biological fact that short-term recall is suppressed during dreaming accounts for some of that dream loss. A lack of interest in dreams is a culprit as well, as in cultures where dreams are regarded as meaningful, more people remember them.

Writers and artists are the outliers here. Some 80 percent of artists and 50 percent of fiction writers say they are affected by their dreams, according to Deirdre Barrett, author of *The Committee of Sleep*. And in *Writers Dreaming*, Naomi Epel chronicles the relationships between two dozen authors from William Styron to Maya Angelou and Amy Tan and their dreams. In his essay "The Symbolic Language of Dreams," Stephen King writes, "Creative imagining and dreaming are just so similar that they've got to be related."

Some familiarity with how the brain works helps us fine-tune our writing habits and invigorate our work. Here are some useful facts about dreaming for writers:

- During REM sleep we are primed for creating random associations. Regions of the brain that produce vivid imagery are highly activated.
- The limbic system, where strong emotions originate, lights up on scans of the dreaming brain. This is a boon to writers, as passionate emotions fuel great literature, too.
- As mentioned previously, areas of the brain that create metaphor are also active when we're dreaming, making REM sleep a garden of poetic possibility.
- Also, thanks to a shift in our sleeping brain's neurochemistry, production of serotonin and norepinephrine is reduced while we dream, meaning that we lose our inhibitions. While the internal censor is dozing, the dreaming mind is free to explore terrain we might consider taboo when awake and we're less likely to nix ideas we would habitually dismiss by day.
- In the nighttime brain, emotions are intensified by the highly activated amygdala, while the dorsal-lateral prefrontal cortex (DLPFC), where rational thought is produced, is largely offline. This sets the scene for creative as well as spiritual epiphanies and provides fodder for dramatic productions on the page, too.[2]

Navigating the Fertile Territory of the In-Between

The French call the liminal space between day and night *l'heure entre chiene et loup*, "the hour between dog and wolf." The phrase references how light changes at dusk and dawn, making it difficult to distinguish a dog from a wolf. It also poetically describes the dreamy muddle between what is domesticated, that is, the dogged demands of waking life versus what is wild and mysterious in the wolf-howling moonlit night.

Prosaically speaking, the scientific term for that middle ground between sleep and dreams is hypnagogia. Hypnopompia describes the moments between sleep and waking. You may have experienced these trippy interludes as you're falling asleep (hypnagogia) or waking up (hypnopompia), when a parade of seemingly random imagery plays out behind your closed eyes as you are hammocked between waking and dreaming consciousness.

Many writers intuit the poetic possibilities of putting pen to paper during those liminal times at the beginning and the end of each day. In *From Where You Dream*, novelist Robert Olen Butler advises writers to go to their desk immediately after waking, to preserve the trancelike state and "dream into your story." In the fluid neurochemical dawn between dog and the wolf, we can access the best of both states of consciousness.

At bedtime, as the dorsal-lateral prefrontal cortex is winding down, and with it our more linear, logical, and ordered ways of thinking, we can tap into the in-between, too. I often write poetry in the hours after bedtime, when the emotionally charged limbic system and parts of the brain that create vivid imagery and random associations are preparing to wake up and come online.

These fluid states of in-between consciousness can be courted and expanded. Some advanced meditation practitioners use focusing techniques to lengthen periods of hypnagogia and hypnopompia so they can maintain awareness as they witness the flow of imagery that appears between sleep and dreams. Some can even remain in a state of conscious awareness through all the sleep stages.

Shamans use drumming and dance to enter hybrid dream states called journeys, where they access information and heal individuals or help the community. Some shamanic journeys also take place during a dream state similar to hypnagogia, hypnopompia, or lucid dreaming, which is another hybrid state of consciousness.

Even without special training, anyone can practice riding the waves of hypnagogia and hypnopompia, or lucid dreaming (the dream state when you are aware that you're dreaming while you are dreaming). Writers may even have an advantage here, as we already have our ways of entering what Butler calls the writer's trance (or what I refer to as the writer's dream) in order to do our work. Pen in hand or fingers poised on keyboards, we shift into an imaginative daydream. Like the lucid dreamer who has some agency within the dream, writers enter and maneuver within the worlds of our characters as if consciously moving within a dream.

Enter the Writer's Dream

Your brain knows how to shift from one state of consciousness to another. After all, our brain moves from light sleep to deep sleep to dreams and back all night long. So, too, we can choose to enter dreamy states of consciousness with these practices:

> **Begin where you are.** Sometimes it happens spontaneously: You dissolve into the poem or story you're composing, barely aware of where you are or that time is passing. Try to observe the subtle shifts you make or techniques you use at times like that as you enter the writer's dream. Are there habits or

activities that help you get there? Take note of what works—and what does not work—for you.

Many ways in. Experiment with different ways to enter the writer's dream at will. Try listening to a guided visualization before writing. (You can find many online, such as those by Anna Wise, author of *The High-Performance Mind* and an expert on creativity and the science of brain waves.) This will help activate theta brain waves—the frequency of electrical impulses measured during dream sleep—to stoke your creativity.

Desk nap. Take a short nap before a writing session or midway through a longer one. Set a timer for about twenty minutes, which is just enough time to hover at the threshold of sleep, without falling into a deep slumber. The aim is to dip into some hypnagogic imagery and activate dreamy brain waves to inspire your creativity—without entering a full-on log-sawing snore-fest.

Linger in the In-Between

Practice recognizing the hypnagogic state between being awake and falling asleep by using this "Light in the Dark Meditation." Done at bedtime, while snuggled under the covers, this *beditation* (meditation in bed) will help you relax and fall asleep. It might also induce lucid dreaming. You can also use this technique as a meditation during the day by using the dreamlets that form behind your closed eyes, rather than your breath, as the object of concentration. Here's how:

1. Get comfortable and close your eyes.
2. Feel your eyelids and eyeballs relax, and keep a soft focus as you observe the inner darkness.
3. Notice that the darkness is not a uniform blackness. There are areas of relative brightness within the darkness. Streaks of light might pass by, and circles of light might form. Colors or images might develop. There's no right or wrong here. Just notice what appears, and stay with it.

4. If thoughts arise, bring your attention back to the light in the darkness, or any shapes or images that form.
5. If a dream begins to form, let it. Observe it and see where it leads, while continuing to remain awake and aware with eyes closed.
6. Do this meditation for as long as feels comfortable. You might start with a minute or two, and add another minute each time. Or, if *beditating*, continue until you fall asleep.

There is no intellect in this world powerful
enough to create a great work of novelistic art.
Only the unconscious can fit together the stuff
of fiction; the conscious mind cannot.

—Robert Olen Butler, *From Where You Dream*

The Midnight Muse

Lydia, one of my dreamwork clients, feared she had a sleeping disorder. "It's so hard for me to switch from dreams to waking life," she told me. "Before noon nothing happens for me," she complained, adding that she felt she was wasting time in the morning when she ought to be more productive.

I suggested that she might just need some quiet time early in the day while her brain chemistry transitioned from the demands of her active dream life to a hectic daytime schedule. The brain's beta waves, the ones that help us with logical, concrete thinking, are in slow supply when we first wake in the morning. Meanwhile, the slow-wave delta and dreamy theta waves may still be plentiful. The ability to work with the flow of our mind's constantly shifting brain chemistry—rather than fight it—can help us live in harmony with our natural rhythms and boost our creativity and productivity.

For writers, this can mean choosing the best time of day for creative activities. Many writers intuit the benefits of writing in the early morning or late at night to access their full creative potential. In his novel *Wonder Boys*, Michael Chabon offers a description of what he calls "the midnight disease," which he has described as a cosmic curse and creative blessing.

In an interview with *The Guardian*, Chabon says, "I work at night, starting at around 10 o'clock and working until 2 or 3 in the morning. I do that usually five days a week." He adds, "It's always been my tendency: working at night just seems quieter and I can focus more easily and the words tends to come more readily."[3]

Toni Morrison's writing habits changed over time as her life circumstances changed. At one point, she did her best writing early in the morning. In the book *Daily Rituals* by Mason Currey, Morrison says:

> Writers devise ways to approach the place where they expect to make the contact, where they become the conduit, or where they engage in this mysterious process. . . . For me, light is the signal in the transaction. It's not being in the light, it's being there before it arrives.

As for Lydia, once she understood that her brain needed time to shift gears, she stopped judging herself as lazy, and instead relaxed into a morning routine that allowed her to wake up slowly. Now she eats a leisurely breakfast and sips a cup of tea while she records her dreams. "I realize my brain is trying to process things, so now my quiet morning routine feels like a productive time, rather than a waste of time," she said.

Whether finding the best time to write, or the optimal times for reflection versus focused attention, knowing the science behind the workings of the brain can help us function better with less effort and more ease.

Find the Right Time to Write

Put your knowledge of brain science to work for you. As an experiment, try writing at a different time of day than usual. Set aside twenty to thirty minutes first thing in the morning or just before bedtime to write. Reflect in your journal about what you notice and what works best for you.

BECAUSE YOU ARE GOING SOMEPLACE: MOVING FROM ROUTINE TO RITUAL

During the Q&A after a standing-room-only literary reading I attended at Smith College, the poet Ocean Vuong was asked if he had a writing ritual. Without missing a beat, he said no, he did not. Then, after a moment's thought, while the students, faculty, and appreciative fans who were packed into the room waited for what he would say next, Vuong backtracked. On second thought, he said—as if he was just discovering something in that moment for himself—he does have one.

"I put on my sneakers before I write," he said. "Because when I write, I'm going someplace."

> When tea becomes ritual, it takes its place at the heart of our ability to see greatness in small things.
>
> —Muriel Barbery, *The Elegance of the Hedgehog*

That moment between the poet's reflexive answer—no, he does not have any rituals—and his flash of self-awareness stayed with me. Often our routines are so, well, *routine* that we barely notice them. We sharpen our pencils before we sit down, even if we'll be writing in pen. Or we listen to Vivaldi on mornings when we write, or we check our social media before opening our story-in-progress.

Like preparing for bed each night, sitting down to write might seem like a mundane activity. But when we bring consciousness to habitual actions, we imbue them with anticipatory energy and a sense of purpose and meaning. In each case, we are, as Vuong said, going someplace: We're crossing a threshold from ordinary day-to-day consciousness into imaginal realms. We are opening doors to unknown territories—and we are reporting back on what we find there.

—

So far, we've explored the connections between dreams and writing, and we've looked through the lenses of history and science to establish why these are such companionable bedfellows. Now we'll look at how to establish some practices that will support your dreamy writing. These can include anything from refreshing your bedtime and waking routines, to consciously setting intentions and living with gratitude, to setting aside a specific time each day to write. We'll identify and acknowledge the rituals you're already engaging in—consciously or not—and create new ones to help sustain and support a vibrant Dreaming on the Page practice.

Make the Mundane Meaningful

The author Ross Gay created a cozy writing ritual for himself—and turned it into a book. Each day for a year he wrote, by hand, about something that delighted him. He kept at it for the length of time it took to finish one cup of coffee—and possibly a refill. After a year, his project was complete. The result is his essay collection, *The Book of Delights*.[4]

As with Gay's example, the best rituals are simple and elegant. You might not even have to add anything to your current routine. Sometimes all that's needed to transform a routine into a ritual is to add a sense of devotion and care to it.

Having a ritual, or a meaningful routine, can support your dream-inspired creativity. Start by recognizing any rituals you might already have:

1. Observe yourself when you begin to write. Do you pour your coffee into the same mug and bring it with you to

your desk each morning? Maybe you turn the lights in your room on in a certain order: first the desk lamp, then the salt lamp, then the overhead light. Do you clear the desk before you begin? Sharpen your pencils? Maybe you check your email before you open your word processing program. You might not know you have a routine, but your subconscious mind picks up subtle clues that signal work is about to begin.

2. Once you identify your routine, discern what's useful and what's not. For example, checking email first never works well for me. I end up answering "just one more," thus cutting into my writing time. But sharpening my pencils is soothing and grounding. This simple concrete task eases me into my writing time.

3. Consider what parts of your routine you can perform consciously, to make your writing time feel more meaningful, satisfying, and productive. A simple action like setting an intention for your writing time when you open your laptop to begin your work, or offering a breath of appreciation for yourself (or your muse) when you close the laptop at the end of your writing session, can be as effective as a more complicated ritual.

4. Something as basic as lighting a candle when you begin to write and blowing it out when you are done can convey to the subconscious mind that whatever doors have opened to emotion, memory, and imagination will now close, so you can return to the tasks of the day. In this way, a ritual can define a boundary between the conscious and unconscious, and it can help contain the uncontainable.

Create a New Ritual

Once you've identified routines you already follow that might easily be elevated to a ritual, you might want to add more. Making up a ritual is a creative act that appeals to many writers because of its soulful and practical benefits. To formalize a ritual for your Dreaming on the Page practice, consider these four elements:

1. Define the space
2. Invite and intend
3. Keep the focus
4. Close up consciously

It's best to start small. Choose one or two of the following suggestions at first. That will be enough to bring new energy and depth to your process on the page.

Define the Space

Room to write. A room of one's own is some writers' ideal—but it's not attainable for everyone. Happily, creating space is not about real estate; it's about designating an area for a specific purpose. Claim a room or a corner of a room as your own, and show up there each day with the intention to write.

Set a boundary. To open the door to writing, you need to close the door on distractions. If your writing room has a door, close it. Let members of your household know that you are not to be interrupted during this time. If you don't have a door, get creative. A novelist I know, whose desk is in the living room, dons a hat when he's writing as a wearable "Do Not Disturb" sign. While you're at it, switch your phones, laptops, and tablets to Do Not Disturb mode during your writing time as well.

Opening action. Light a candle; clear your desk; spritz some energizing rosemary, peppermint, or citrus essential oils into the room; or arrange the items on your desk. Even picking up a pen, or positioning your fingers on the keyboard, if done consciously, can carry the power of ritual. These small gestures function to acknowledge that you are entering a creative space—both physically and mentally.

Invite and Intend

Before you begin to write, set an intention. This affirmative statement should orient you toward how you want to feel and the purpose you want to serve *(Today I'll write with joy for the benefit of all who read my words)* as opposed to a goal, which points toward an accomplishment *(Today I'll write five hundred words)*. Both have their place, but we too often overlook the inner qualities and aspirations we want to bring to our work, and instead focus on tangible, quantifiable goals. You can also take a moment to welcome your characters. Wish them a good morning and tell them you look forward to hearing what they have to say. Why not? Plenty of great writers do! Or visualize your writing role models and ask for their help. (Pictures of Virginia Woolf, Louisa May Alcott, and Walt Whitman, among others, adorn my writing space.)

Move inside. Don't just clear clutter from your desk before you get to work—clear your mind, too. Inhale and observe what's happening inside you, then exhale and let go of anything that might be holding you back.

The quickest slow-speed way to start for busy writers. If you love the idea of creating a writing ritual, but barely have time to write let alone add more things to do, try this technique to quickly settle into the sanctuary of your dreamy mind:

1. Get comfortable in your writing space and take three breaths to ground yourself and turn inward.
2. Place your hands, palms down, on your knees.
3. Slowly draw your hands along your thighs toward your hip creases. Can you make this movement last for three to five full and leisurely breaths?
4. Notice how your mind grows quiet and still as the slow movement reaches its conclusion.
5. When your hands meet your hip creases, turn your palms faceup, and gently open your eyes. You're ready to write.

Keep the Focus

Use a touchstone. A smooth, palm-sized rock I picked up during a writer's retreat rests atop a bookshelf in my study. Each time I see it, I remember how its sun-warmed heft felt nestled in my hand when I picked it up during the closing circle on the last day of the retreat. I slipped the stone into my pocket as a reminder to carve out time and space for my creative work when I returned home. Since then, it has become a literal touchstone, reminding me of my promise to myself. Any object that you imbue with meaning can serve the same purpose: A figurine, a mouse pad imprinted with a meaningful image, or a pen that a writing friend or mentor gave to you can become a touchstone to remind you of your intentions.

Create a soundscape. Playing the same style of music (raga, reggae, jazz, R&B, classical, or a soundtrack that matches the decade your novel is set in, for example) each time you write can literally help you tune into your work. Music without lyrics works best for most writers. For years I listened to baroque music to get into a relaxed and aware mental state for writing. To this day when I hear Bach's cello suites, I have the urge to drop into a chair and pick up my pen.

Close Up Consciously

Goodbye and thank you. To mark the end of your writing time, choose a concluding gesture. You might turn off the music, snap your laptop shut, or put your coffee mug in the sink. Whatever gesture you choose, take a conscious breath as you do it and thank any guides you invited or invoked, or just appreciate yourself—and your characters—for showing up at the page.

Create your blessings. Carol, a DOTP workshop participant, spent several years writing about a family member's addiction and mental illness. Moving into that story each day involved some emotional heavy lifting. To take care of herself in the process, she established a ritual of opening and closing her writing time with a blessing. This simple act sustained her so she could move into the grief and sadness while she wrote and leave it behind when she was through. "The process of writing my memoir brought up a lot of intense feelings. I needed a way to transition from writing to doing other things," Carol explained.

Using Carol's example, create your own blessings or poems to mark the beginning and end of your writing time.

BEDTIME

Fluffy pillows. Soft sheets. A cozy blanket. There's no place we'd rather be at the end of the day than in our bed. In contrast to the rest of our day, the bed is a place to *be*, not *do*.

Or, perhaps that's the problem. According to the Centers for Disease Control and Prevention, despite how we might wax poetic about the allure of falling into bed at the end of the day, sleeplessness in the United States has reached and surpassed epidemic proportions. Maybe it's our addiction to *do*ing and a latent fear of *be*ing that prevents us from embracing the darkness, the stillness, and the quiet that is required for deep rest. Our underlying fears of the dark can also keep us from dreaming—at night and on the page.

> There is a time for many words,
> and there is also a time for sleep.
>
> —Homer, *The Odyssey*

There isn't always a quick and easy fix for this problem. Feeling safe and cared for at bedtime isn't a given for all of us. The darkness holds real dangers for people who have experienced childhood abuse, partner abuse, lived in violent neighborhoods or war-torn countries, or experienced any form of trauma—ancestral or personal.

If you are uncomfortable with the nighttime, you are not alone. Trust your feelings and treat yourself with kindness.

My own fear of the dark began early on. Growing up in a household ruled by my father's unpredictable anger contributed to me becoming an anxious child. I couldn't fall asleep unless my mother left the hall light on and my bedroom door ajar. During my teenage and early adult years, I learned to drown out my fears at bedtime with television noise. But dreams, which have fascinated me through it all, have been my motivation to muster up the courage to turn out the lights and enter the dark. Thanks to a knowledgeable and caring therapist I began working with in college, I learned to use dreams and even nightmares as my practice ground. Working with active imagination and lucid dreaming, I learned to face my monsters and develop the confidence I needed to square my shoulders and face challenges by day, too. Paradoxically, dreams, with their sometimes-disturbing scenarios, can be the reason to avoid bed—or the incentive to seek out sleep and dreams so we can heal our fears.

Bedtime Story

If you have trouble devoting time to sleep, ask yourself what is preventing you from claiming your right to rest? What must you do to make it *to* and *into* your bed? What must you stop doing? What must you shed? Consider your early experiences and beliefs about bedtime by writing in your journal or by sharing with a trusted friend or therapist. For some of us this can be uncomfortable or downright scary territory.

So, be gentle with yourself when you consider the questions that follow. Parcel out brief sessions of five to twenty minutes to do this reflection. Get cozy. Wrap yourself in a blanket or shawl, prepare a cup of sweet-smelling tea, and/or bring along any comforting presences in the form of photos of a loved one or anything else that makes you feel safe when you sit down to write. Then, consider these prompts:

- Write about your bedtime routine when you were five or nine or fourteen. For example, did your family gather to read a story or say a prayer at bedtime when you were small? As a school-age child, did you have time to yourself after lights-out to read a book beneath your covers using a flashlight? As you got older, did you watch a favorite TV show with your siblings before getting ready for bed? What else?

- Did you look forward to going to bed at those ages, or did you dread it? Did you experience something in between? Write about it.
- Write about a memorable dream or a series of recurring dreams. How did your dreams (or lack of them) relate to what was happening in your waking life?
- Look back at what you've written. What have you learned about your early relationship to sleep and dreams? Keep writing.

LISTENING ON THE PAGE

"What brings you here?"

I was eighteen years old, seated in the office of my first therapist. There were so many things that had brought me to that rambling converted Victorian that housed a bevy of therapists' offices in the college town where I lived. But what answer could I offer to this stranger? Was it my father's chronic angry outbursts that had brought me here? My distracted mother's failure to intervene? Their divorce? All I knew was that in my first months away from home, I could no longer ignore the roiling pit of sadness deep inside. Essentially, what brought me there was my entire life up to that moment. But how could I explain that to this petite woman dressed casually in corduroy slacks and a turtleneck sweater, with a practical short haircut to match?

"I guess I just want someone to listen to me," I finally said.

> It's that being open—not scratching for it, not digging for it, not constructing something, but being open to the situation and trusting that what you don't know will be available to you.
>
> **—Toni Morrison, Nobel Prize laureate**

I glanced up at my therapist. Her face communicated an authentic, no-nonsense sincerity.

"Okay," she said gently. "We have an hour. Talk to me. I'm listening." She cocked her head and looked as though she really wanted to hear what I had to say.

And then. I froze. Faced with genuine interest and concern, and with time to express myself and be heard, I was speechless.

Everyone, it seems, is looking for "a good listener." It's one of the top qualities that employers, singles on dating websites, and people seeking friendship say they want. Listening, it turns out, is a rare gift. Perhaps it's so rare that when we finally encounter someone who is ready to hear us, we don't always know what to do. Speaking when we are really being listened to takes practice.

In my writing workshops, I often lead pairs of students in an active listening exercise: The first speaker gets three minutes to talk about the assigned topic—fathers, for example. The other student is instructed to listen without interrupting, and with a mental and physical posture of patient, curious, nonjudgmental, loving attention. Even if the speaker stops talking, her partner is instructed to maintain the same engaged, silent, and attentive posture. What's trickiest, my students tell me, are the silences. After even a few seconds of quiet, inevitably students begin to squirm, giggle, or break the no-crosstalk rule. Afterward they tell me that it was uncomfortable to listen and to be listened to. But then they ask if we can do the exercise again. Despite the difficulties, they crave the experience of truly listening—and of being heard.

It's a little like that trust game where you fall backward into someone's arms. The hopeful voice needs a reliable listener, and the listener has to be ready to receive the weight of what is about to fall into their arms. It's scary because there's always the possibility that the other person will step away, and you'll get hurt. So, we practice building trust.

But I'm not training therapists. I'm a writing teacher. So, we transfer this skill of engaged listening to our process on the page. As dreamers and writers, we benefit from learning to listen skillfully so we can receive information from our dreams, from our imagination, and from different parts of ourselves. I was influenced in my approach to teaching writing as an act of hearing during my studies with Linda Trichter Metcalf, PhD, author and founder, with Tobin Simon, PhD, of the proprioceptive writing method, a meditative writing practice, as described in their book

Writing the Mind Alive: The Proprioceptive Method for Finding Your Authentic Voice.

Public speaking is taught in various settings—active and engaged listening should be, too. We need to become comfortable with the silences where meaning is being constructed and inner discoveries are being made. Our conversations with one another and with ourselves on the page require the same kind of patient, curious, nonjudgmental, and loving attention that I first experienced in the office of my first therapist, decades ago.

Patient, Curious, Nonjudgmental, Loving Attention

Cat, a nineteen-year-old single mother in one of my writing classes, once asked: "What if we spoke the way that we write?"

I had been teaching writing to Cat and her classmates (teen mothers who were studying for their GEDs) the way I always do, by starting with a lesson on how to listen to each other as I described earlier. Then we moved to listening to what we wrote, as we wrote, with the same quality of attention that we used when we listened to one another.

Now, as we absorbed Cat's question, the room that was usually filled with the sounds of students' voices contradicting, arguing, opining, and competing to be heard above the din grew quiet. Writing in this new way inspired integrity so that the writer's thoughts, beliefs, and words fell into alignment. It fostered responses born of contemplation and resisted knee-jerk reactions. Now we were following Cat's train of thought: What if we practiced that level of integrity when we spoke to one another in the classroom—and beyond?

For the rest of that day, and more and more that semester, our spoken conversations began to resemble the thoughtful paragraphs we were composing on the page.

Listening to ourselves and one another with patient, curious, nonjudgmental, loving attention is a game changer. Now, let's break that list down:

Patient. Listen as though you have nowhere else to be. Wait for what will come next, without trying to control it. It helps to be present and relaxed in your body and your mind. Notice if you are poised to challenge, change, argue, or agree with what you're hearing. If so, take a breath, pause, and let go of planning your response. You're not necessarily condoning or concurring with what you're hearing—you are simply receiving a story as it unfolds, for as long as it takes.

Curious. When we're curious, we want to know more. We're focused. What else is there to this story? Why does this person believe what they believe? What evidence do they have for their point of view? Get curious about your reactions to what you're hearing, too. Why did you drift off just then? When did you start to feel resistance? What provoked your mind chatter to start up again?

Nonjudgmental. Evaluating whether something is good or bad, acceptable to you or not, jolts you out of the story that's being told—and it pulls you away from the present moment. To be nonjudgmental, foster a state of open receptivity. When you notice that you're judging, you've taken the first step to being a nonjudgmental listener. Reset your intention, and try again to hear what is being said.

Loving. Adding the word *loving* to this list is redundant, because when we listen with patient, curious, nonjudgmental attention, it is, in effect, an act of love. But I include the word *loving* here because it's worth repeating.

Listening in this way requires us to be vulnerable and open— and that's not easy. Which is why we may resist doing it, and why we need to practice daily. When we do, we are rewarded with the gift of vibrancy, depth, and fresh perspective as we listen to one another, our dreams, and our thoughts on and off the page.

I share all your prejudices against dream interpretation as the quintessence of uncertainty and arbitrariness. On the other hand, I know that if we meditate on a dream sufficiently long and thoroughly, if we carry it around with us and turn it over and over, something almost always comes of it.

—Carl Jung, Swiss psychiatrist

Turning Dreams Over. And Over: Writing as Noninterpretive Dreamwork

Meaning. We hunger for it.

We want to know the meaning of life and what our partner means when they say "I love you." We want to know what the ending of the movie means, and the meaning of song lyrics. But when it comes to poetry and dreams, our search for meaning can end in bafflement and frustration—when what we are seeking is satisfaction—if not enlightenment.

But perhaps "What does it mean?" is the wrong question. Think back to your seventh-grade English class. Your teacher likely offered you a poem and asked you what it means. And that was the beginning of the end of your love of poetry. Because, until that moment, the strange combination of words and images arranged on jaunty lines had excited you. You had been transported to the cold, slippery rocks of a distant beach, and the salt spray of the crashing waves tasted like tears on your cheeks. Until the teacher demanded that you tell the class what the poem means. You couldn't put your feelings into words and you weren't sure what the right answer was, so you said something you thought the teacher wanted to hear, and all the dazzlement went out of it.

Maybe she praised you. Maybe she started to talk about meter and rhyme, simile and metaphor, and suddenly the tumultuous pull of the stormy sea and the hunger in your heart shriveled up like a starfish beached on the sand. Math class was more appealing than this, and you don't even like math.

With all due respect (and most deserve bouquets of respect) to seventh-grade English teachers, this is no way to introduce someone to a poem. And it's certainly no way to introduce twelve- and thirteen-year-olds to poetry.

We have a similar problem with dreams. I suspect that the reason a lot of people shy away from paying attention to their dreams is that they don't know what they mean—and they desperately want to know! How desperately? The phrase *dream interpretation* is typed into the Google search bar (our modern-day oracle) 100,000 to one million times a month (which is about ten times more than people searched for a sourdough bread recipe during the COVID-19 pandemic, for example). But a search engine can't interpret your dream for you. And neither can I. Even Carl G. Jung, the grandfather of modern dreamwork, said that when someone told him a dream, his first thought was something along the lines of "I have no idea what that dream means, either."

And yet, I'm a dreamworker who is asked daily to interpret people's dreams. And I teach poetry to people who don't consider themselves to be poets. That means I spend a lot of time trying to convince people that they'll enjoy the whole experience more if they give themselves a pass on pinning down meaning.

One of the first things I did when I began teaching poetry to adults and young adults in literacy settings was to ditch the whole "what does this poem mean?" business. Shakespeare's "wandering bark," Dickinson's "mechanical feet" going round on their "wooden way," and Lorca's direct address to the color green were baffling to my students—as they were to me the first several times I'd encountered them. Instead, I suggested we listen to poems as if they were music. You don't need to understand a song to be moved by it, after all.

After we read the poem aloud once or twice, I might ask: "What do you feel when you hear this poem?" "What do you see or smell when you hear it?" "What does it make you wonder about?" And then I might ask: "Any idea why someone would have written this to begin with?"

Because, do we really want to know what a poem *means*? We want it to inspire us, to challenge us, inform and entertain us. We want it to make us somehow fuller, better, braver. We want a poem to move us. We want the poem to feel as if we wrote it; we want it to become part of us. We want it to express something we didn't even know needed expression—but now that we hear it, we do need it. It has become essential to us, whether for a moment or for a lifetime. We want to know what a poem means to *us*.

I like poet Matthew Zapruder's anti-interpretation approach to poetry. Writing about the Slovenian poet Tomaz Salamun in an article in the *New York Times*, Zapruder says, "[His] poems are not designed to be interpreted but instead to act upon us, in order to open up in us a little dormant space of weirdness where we can hopefully feel more free."[5] Yes! A little (liberating) dormant space of weirdness. That is something a poem can offer us if we don't force it into the corset of interpretation.

Instead of interpreting poems with my students, we spend time with them. We allow them to be inscrutable. We allow ourselves to feel confused and confounded. We wallow around within the tangled lines until we find a word or phrase that stirs something within us. We tug on that strand, and follow it to the next moment of connection. Then we read the poem aloud again. We might abandon it for a time and then return to it. And, at some point, sometimes sooner and sometimes much later, the poem begins to interpret itself. It opens to us, and we find many meanings within it—meanings that may shift and change over time.

It's the same with dreams. A dream isn't meant to be deciphered like a message tapped out in Morse code, any more than a poem is. It's more like a soft-bellied being that retreats to its shell if we poke and prod at it. It's a fish that will swim out of reach if we try to grab it. A dream is like a cat. It's best to sit still and let it come to us.

Jung wrote that for the artist to experience and understand "the images, symbols, and visions that rise up from the depths; [they] must assimilate and integrate them actively." *Assimilate and integrate* means to take them inside oneself, listen to them, embody them, and discover where they live in us.

A client of mine had been having dreams of finding pieces of paper inscribed with words in a foreign alphabet. In dream after dream, she tried to decipher their meaning. She expressed her frustration at not knowing what the words—and the dreams—meant. Until finally, in one dream, she picked up the pages and, rather than strain to translate the text, she pressed pages directly into her heart—until she felt full.

We can read dreams with our hearts by taking them in without needing to understand every—or any—image they offer. We can journal our dreams, make poems from our dreams, or write them out in the second or third person as if they are stories (which, it turns out, they are). Somewhere along the way, as you are describing the iguana crawling across the bottom of the swimming pool from last night's dream, you will sense the emptiness you feel inside. You now see what you've been avoiding for weeks: You've been crawling, belly-down, across the cracked cement bottom of the parched well of your creativity. Describing the iguana, a creature who knows how to survive a dry spell, you realize it has something to teach you. As you keep writing, you enter a current of curiosity that courses just beneath your skin. You swim with it. For the first time in a long time, you're in the flow.

When you know that my poems are not poems
Then we can speak of poetry!

—Ryokan, Buddhist monk

Let Your Dreams Interpret Themselves

It's easy to rush through the process of writing down dreams. We want to catch every detail and we don't have much time before the rest of the world wakes up and the demands of our family members, colleagues, or to-do lists take over. Do it anyway: Listen to your dreams. They have something to say to you, and with patience, you'll begin to understand their language. Here are some tips and reminders:

Speed limit. Write slowly and notice how you feel as you write. Are there parts of the dream that make you anxious? Which parts make you sigh? Where in your body do you feel something? Keep your focus anchored to what you are experiencing. (If you don't have time to write the entire dream slowly, write even the first line or two with an attitude of timeless, patient immersion. As in all things dream-related, a small act of intention and attention goes a long way.)

Listen with love. When someone tells you a dream, they are sharing something from deep within themselves. The same is true when you tell yourself a dream by writing it down. So, give your dream the gift of your undivided attention. When you're not sure what to write next, pause. Stay engaged with the silences between your thoughts—until you know what to write next.

No need to understand. Let it be okay *not* to know. You don't need to understand dreams. Instead, appreciate their creativity, uniqueness, or even bizarreness!

Ask, don't tell. Rather than try to interpret a dream or decipher what it means, ask open-ended questions that don't dead-end into yes-or-no answers. You might ask: "What does this dream make me think about?" "How does it make me feel?" And "What might it be trying to tell me?"

Make It Joyful

Just as straining to interpret a dream "correctly" drains the joy from it, so, too, can trying too hard to follow all the steps and guidance in this section. Consider the various tips and techniques offered, then try one or two at a time. The means, in this case, *are* the ends. So, make your time with yourself joyful and celebratory whenever you can.

> **Less is more**. Prioritize the quality of your time with dreams and writing over the quantity. Adopt one technique or suggestion at a time, and if you start to feel overwhelmed, pause. As dreamers, we honor our need for rest.
>
> **Recognize yourself**. Every day that you spend five minutes or more consciously connecting with your dreams and/or writing, acknowledge yourself for doing it. Go ahead, give yourself a gold star; share your accomplishment with an accountability partner; or put a dollar in an envelope—then at the end of the week or month, use that cash to buy yourself a treat (a cuppa something foamy and delicious, or a special new journal or pen works for me!).
>
> **Create community**. Find a few dreamy friends and start a Dreaming on the Page circle. Get together in person or online to write, share dreams, and support each other on the journey. (For more on how to start a DOTP circle, see Circles of Connection, beginning on page 224.)

Part Two

THE GENERATIVE DREAM: EXERCISES TO JUMP-START YOUR WRITING

Now that you've been filling your notebook with dream reports, it's time to revisit them—this time as repositories of raw material for your writing. This section will function like a Dreaming on the Page workshop in a book. Here you'll find a set of foundational practices followed by lessons on various aspects of dreams and writing designed to activate your imagination. As a result, you'll experience your dreaming mind as a generous wellspring of inspiration.

> To write is to feel the dance of your soul swirling in a dream that drips imagination onto paper.
>
> —DiAnn Mills, *The Dance of Character and Plot*

You can use the material in this section in a variety of ways. For example, you can use the prompts as warm-ups before you launch into a larger writing project, or just to get your creative juices flowing before starting your daily routines; to inspire new pieces of writing; or to explore and deepen the characters, themes, and plots you are already writing about. There is much to be gained from returning to a prompt again and again, each time applying it to a different dream, and each time finding new inspiration in it.

A Workshop That Works for You

I teach Dreaming on the Page workshops as half-day events, or as weekend-long or eight-week courses. That means that most lessons are designed as stand-alone activities that can be mixed and matched and completed in any order. So, complete the exercises in this section in the way that works for you. Sample one lesson or prompt at a time—or binge on a whole batch at once. You can move from the beginning to the end of the section in order, or, if you prefer, skip around among the lessons using your intuition as a guide. Here are some suggestions to help you to have a sustainable, productive, and nourishing DOTP experience:

Make a date with yourself. You can start working with these exercises anytime, but when you do, it's best to make a regular appointment with yourself each week, preferably on the same day or days (Wednesday and Saturday mornings, for example), to devote to the Dreaming on the Page lessons. Consistency will prime your subconscious mind to be ready when it's time to dream into your writing.

Get grounded. As I mentioned earlier, these exercises can be completed in or out of order. However, I suggest you start by moving through the foundational practices that lead off this section. That will give you a solid grounding in some DOTP basics and enhance your experience as you progress through the lessons.

Take your time. In addition to prompts, I've offered example texts to inspire your writing. When you can, spend a few minutes reading and rereading the excerpts provided, notice what works for you about the author's writing, and then use the prompt to generate a poem, story, or journal entry of your own.

Pause, then continue. Before moving on to the next lesson, you might want to review, reflect on, or revise what you've written. You can even try the prompt(s) on another dream before moving on to the next exercises. Do what feels right for you.

Be accountable. The freedom of doing a workshop on your own schedule is liberating, but it can also help to have an accountability partner. Invite a friend to join you in your DOTP journey. Text, email, or call one another each week to check in, read to one another from what you've written, or just to encourage one another to keep going. Or, be your own accountability partner. At the end of each writing session, mark off your achievement on your calendar with a star or another symbol to track your progress. And take a moment to appreciate your accomplishment.

A Note on the Example Texts

The excerpts from works of poetry, fiction, and nonfiction included with these lessons are meant to inspire your own writing. Although the lines I've chosen are all you need to complete the exercise, I encourage you to find a copy of the full text so you can deepen your experience and learn even more. Just about all the texts I've included are easily accessible in their entirety online. For those that are not, you can order the books referenced through your local library or favorite bookseller. You can even devote a special shelf for your Dreaming on the Page–themed books.

We are about to begin. So, turn the page and prepare to discover new and creative ways to combine dreams and writing. Let's get started!

FOUNDATIONAL
PRACTICES

> *Immature poets imitate, mature poets steal.*
>
> —T. S. Eliot, poet

Of Pearls, Pebbles, and Prompts

I arrive for the first day of most writing workshops carrying a small orange tote bag embroidered with silver and red blossoms and stuffed with everyday objects: a wooden spool, a pocket comb, a paper clip, a small plastic truck, a house key, a toy soldier, a thimble.

When the group has settled in and is ready to write, I pass the bag around and ask each participant to reach in and grab something. "Don't peek!" I say. "Let yourself be surprised." Once everyone has an item in hand, I instruct them to contemplate it: "Notice its shape, texture, and weight. What associations, stories, or memories come to mind?"

Then it's time to write.

What happens next never ceases to amaze me. Whether it's a group of writers who've had long experience publishing poems and stories, a group of dreamers at a conference who don't think of themselves as writers at all, or a classroom full of teen mothers studying for their high school equivalency exam, each participant puts down their pen at the end of our writing time and shares a poem or story that warms, startles, compels, or moves us.

This is the power of the humble writing prompt.

A prompt is nothing more than a suggestion a group leader offers at the start of a five-, ten-, or twenty-minute writing period to help writers bypass self-consciousness and steer clear of well-worn ruts. They usually take the form of sentence starters, such as *I remember . . .* or *I am from . . .* , that launch writers into original narrative terrain. An object, like one pulled from my embroidered tote, can serve as a prompt as well. Whatever form they take, prompts are so ubiquitous in writing groups that we seldom think about why they so reliably help us overcome whatever resistances might be keeping us stuck and open troves of creative treasures.

I believe prompts are a boon to creativity because they imitate the actions of the dreaming mind. To simplify a complex biological process, when we sleep and dream, the brain stem fires random neuronal impulses. The narrative-loving mind responds to these flashes of image, memory, or emotion by wrapping stories around them—resulting in the cryptic and captivating dreams we experience each night.

But I'm a poet, not a scientist. Although I'm fascinated by facts, I'm drawn in by fictions that convey complicated truths. So, I imagine the prompt as a pebble tossed into the waters of the writer's mind. Arriving unexpectedly and seemingly out of the blue, this nugget splashes through the surface, and ripples of possibility radiate from it.

Or, I like to think of my mind as an oyster and the prompt falls, like a grain of sand, into its soft belly. That granular intrusion triggers a reaction, and a pearl (of poetry or prose) is formed.

Either way, I welcome the writing prompt as part of a creative ecosystem like the one that our dreaming brain creates for us each night, when a neuronal impulse catalyzes a dream into being.

Prompt: DIY Writing Prompts

You don't have to wait for a teacher to supply a prompt. Just tune into your dreams for a steady stream of nighttime creativity boosters. Here's how:

1. Review a collection of your dreams, and underline three to five intriguing, inventive, or surprising lines or phrases.
2. Copy the Dream Lines onto slips of paper and keep them in a special box or envelope on your writing desk.
3. When you're stuck, randomly select one of your Dream Lines and use it as a prompt to guide your writing.
4. Alternatively, you can select three or more Dream Lines at random and rearrange them into a poem or the start of a story.

> *The first step to being a writer is to hitch the unconscious mind to your writing arm.*
>
> —Dorothea Brande, *Becoming a Writer*

In the Subconscious Mind We Trust: Building a Relationship That Works

The first time I sat in a writing circle with Patricia Lee Lewis, an elegant woman with a lilting Texas accent, she told a story that made me wonder whether she was kooky or brilliant. During a solo cross-country adventure, in a situation where others would rely on maps and guidebooks, Lewis packed a pendulum. She decided where to camp and which direction to set off in based on whether the weighted pendant hanging from a chain swung back and forth or in circles, communicating either a yes or a no.

As it turns out, this anecdote illustrated the philosophy Lewis uses to guide her writing and her pedagogy as a teacher. Just as she trusted that pendulum to determine which road to follow and where to pitch her tent, she also encourages her students to trust their subconscious minds to lead their writing along the path it needs to take.

Over the years that I've studied and taught with Lewis, she has been a role model for me. Her example helped me renew my faith in my own commitment to nurturing a relationship with my dreams, intuition, and creativity—and to value writing as an art form that brings them all together.

Prompt: Make a Contract with Your Subconscious

In *Zen in the Art of Writing*, Ray Bradbury emphasizes the importance of the writer developing a healthy relationship with the subconscious mind. How? By having faith in your intuition and dreams. To practice this, decide that each morning this week you'll take the first words or dream image you wake up thinking about and put them into your writing.

By now you should have a pen and paper beside your bed. Use them to jot down a line or image from your dreamy mind in the morning. Then write:

1. *I woke with this word or image today:* _____
2. When you get to your desk, set your timer for four to seven minutes and begin to write.
3. Insert your word into your piece before the timer chimes.
4. That's it: You've kept your contract with the subconscious— and you've added a flash of the unexpected to your writing.

Even if what you write using this prompt seems silly or unproductive at first, stick with it and see where it leads. The trick is to honor the relationship between your conscious and subconscious mind. When you do, you build your intuitive muscles and strengthen the bond between your inner and outer selves.

Material Wealth

I stumbled, quite by accident, into a career as a writing instructor. At age thirty-one, I left my job as a journalist (but not my need to pay a mortgage) to indulge my dream of getting an MFA in creative writing. The only work-study job I could find that fit my schedule was teaching poetry with the Teachers and Writers Collaborative in the New York City public schools. With no previous training and no relevant degree, I started teaching K-12 students and went on to teach teen mothers in high school equivalency programs and refugees and immigrants in English as a second language classes. I had a lot to learn—and quickly. After all, the stakes were high: The students I was working with had experienced poverty, trauma, and violence resulting from systems of inequality and injustice. Not surprisingly, it wasn't easy for them to open up on the page.

That meant that I needed a crash course in finding ways to break through students' resistance to seeing themselves as writers. And I needed to find a patch of common ground where we could meet—despite our vastly different circumstances and backgrounds so we could connect and create.

Asking students about their dreams became one way in. Many had strong opinions about what dreams mean or don't mean. Or they might have had a friend or family member whose dreams seem to tell the future. Or they themselves have had an experience of a deceased parent or uncle or aunt revealing family secrets in a dream. The information and points of view varied widely, but the stories of and about dreams kept us all riveted and wanting to know more. Now we had found some common ground, and all we had to do was make the transition from telling stories to writing them down. Everything, it seemed, went more smoothly after that.

I began to build confidence—not at first in myself or my teaching methods, but in the fact that, despite everything, these students had within them poems and stories that were alive with metaphor and meaning, and they were tumbling out onto the page. It wasn't just some of them who wowed us with their words, but every single student did—and there have been hundreds, if not thousands, in my classes over the decades.

I couldn't even try to boast that it was my teaching prowess that was responsible. Instead, this experience confirmed that poetry is not an esoteric exercise for the elite. My work for the past decade-plus as a professional dreamworker, hearing as many dream reports as newly minted poems and stories, has backed that up. Our creative minds churn out stories at a rate that outperforms even the most prolific writer. These two realizations became twin beams that have illuminated my path as I've continued to build a career teaching in nontraditional settings—and when teaching nontraditional topics, such as dream studies. Put it all together, and we're dreaming on the page.

When working with adults and young adults who say they can't—or won't—write, and whose imaginations have been sealed shut by the shock of abuse and trauma, dreams provide a welcoming ambassador to the literary imagination. They can step in as amanuensis, feeding us lines as we take dictation from the creative director of the night so that we have fodder for the page. I've even tweaked the Zimbabwean proverb: "If you can walk, you can dance; if you can talk, you can sing." My version goes like this: "If you dream, you can write."

Before my students even have a chance to say they have nothing to write, I remind them: "Write down a dream." Pencils scratch, then skitter, then fly across the page.

Prompt: Be the Secretary of Dreams

Bolstered anew by the conviction that creativity is our birthright, let's look at prompts I use with my students to make creative writing as easy as taking dictation. And don't worry, no short-hand skills are needed. Here's how:

1. Write a dream in the present tense, as if the events in the dream are happening now.
2. Let the dream speak for itself. Leave out any exposition, interpretation, or commentary.
3. Employ the same level of attention to detail and description you'd put into writing a story or poem. Replace tired words or phrases with vivid ones. Choose strong nouns and verbs that conjure up specific imagery and actions.
4. After you've taken dictation from your dream, edit lightly. Take out unnecessary words and, if writing a poem, insert line breaks.
5. Reread your piece one more time. Delight in the poem or story you've created—with a little help from your dreams!

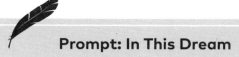

Prompt: In This Dream

Choose a few random images and actions from a dream and write them out as a list (for example, your list might include a preacher with long braids addressing an outdoor congregation in a grim neighborhood; a set of wooden stairs appearing out of nowhere; strange weeds springing up on the lawn). Then insert the phrase *In this dream* before each item from your list. For example:

> In this dream a preacher with long braids addresses a congregation in the open air of a grim neighborhood
>
> In this dream a wooden staircase appears out of nowhere
>
> In this dream strange weeds spring up in the field . . .

See where your list takes you. Is there the start of a poem or story here? Keep writing.

If what we need to dream, to move our spirits most deeply and directly toward and through promise, is a luxury, then we have given up the core—the fountain—of our power . . . we have given up the future of our worlds.

—Audre Lorde, "Poetry Is Not a Luxury"

Blocked: On the Page and on the Pillow

Deshawn, a seventh grader, shot his hand into the air after I'd given the day's writing prompt. "Miss!" he called out. "I can't do it. I have writer's blank!"

Even now when my fingers hover, frozen, above the keyboard, this memory softens my resistance to the soul-numbing condition otherwise known as writer's block and makes me smile. Often that's enough to unstick the gears and get me writing again.

As awful as writer's block (or blank) is for a seventh grader writing poetry in language arts class, it can be far worse for a professional writer under pressure to produce on the page, or a novelist or poet whose creativity won't flow.

Victoria Nelson highlighted the role of the unconscious in these stubborn stoppages in her book *Writer's Block*:

> Although it can be triggered by any number of internal or external stimuli, the vital function that writer's block performs during the creative process remains constant: inability to write means that the unconscious self is vetoing the program demanded by the conscious ego.

The term *writer's block* was coined in 1947 by Freudian psychiatrist Edmund Bergler, who (unsurprisingly in light of his training) saw it as a form of neurosis stemming from a frustrated infantile longing for the free flow of mother's milk. While most of us today would reject that theory, he may have been onto an archetypal association. In her book *The Moon and the Virgin,* Nor Hall suggests that, according to myth, soul blockages (which can manifest as anything from infertility to artistic blocks) could mean that a goddess is blocking the doorway with her arms and legs crossed in refusal. To appease her, a ritual of untying knots (shoelaces, bows and ribbons, tangled necklaces) and opening and unlocking doors and windows was prescribed to let the creative (or procreative) energies flow freely again.

Interestingly, there is no corollary term for dreamer's block, but that condition can be just as dispiriting during a spell of low or no dream recall. Perhaps because dreaming doesn't serve the pursuit of prestige, commercial gain, or academic advancement, dream droughts are rarely acknowledged. But writer's block and dream loss are both real and connected.

Both writing and dreaming require that we dwell in the uneasy darkness of uncomfortable thoughts and feelings. This is a vulnerable stance that requires surrender to the unknown. Still and quiet in the dark, awaiting sleep, we close our eyes and open to the possibility of either pleasant dreams or nightmares, with little say over which we'll experience. Still and quiet at our desk, enveloped in solitude, we open the door to the story we plan to tell—knowing that any number of unwanted stories that we've long been avoiding may sashay through that unguarded doorway, too.

Still and quiet: It is an uneasy combination. We pack our schedules and keep our phones within arm's reach at all times for a reason. In *The Life of Poetry*, poet Muriel Rukeyser names the problem: We fear poetry because we fear emotions. Like Deshawn, by age fourteen most of us have learned there's no guarantee of safety, but we try to fortify ourselves against hurt anyway. Wandering into the wilds of memory and imagination, we risk recalling painful memories or discovering aspects of ourselves that don't fit into the petty roles proscribed for us by our families, peer groups, or societal expectations. We are not raised to be fluent in the felt alphabet of our emotions.

Poetry, in its abstract foreignness and refusal to obey the logic of linear thought, is regarded with suspicion or outright contempt by the dominant culture. So is any attempt at expression that peels away our masks of certainty. It's the collective dread of our tenuous grasp on life on its own terms that holds us back. It's the fear of digging, bare-handed, into the mud of grievances and griefs long hidden.

That's why when I teach, I keep a box of tissues on the table. Even the most innocuous writing prompt such as *Describe the contents of your mother's pocketbook*, or a seemingly mundane dream when spoken out loud, might uncork an unexpected stream of tears. I've had high school students who are required to be in my poetry classes say they hate writing, when soon enough it becomes clear that what they are really saying is that it's scary. It's also why I'm not surprised when dream clients, after a particularly productive session, cancel the next one. As Carl Jung has written, "One does not become enlightened by imaginary figures of light, but by making the darkness conscious."

We avoid what we don't understand by clinging to well-known and well-worn worrying thoughts—as if this tangled rope of anxiety could save us from the discomfort of the unpredictable future or the unresolved past. Even those of us—you, for example—who are sold on dreamwork and writing may hesitate to fearlessly enter the uncharted regions of the imaginal realms. This quote, attributed to Anne Lamott, says it well: "My mind is like a bad neighborhood, I try not to go there alone." Ultimately, though, walking freely along those streets is our birthright. And once we learn how to do so safely, it's worth every step.

True, opening to the unknown when we sleep, dream, and write isn't easy. But building a capacity to do so is essential if we want to wander unfettered through our own minds and hearts. When we do, we find our own truths and enjoy the freedom to write and dream into the stories that are ours to tell.

Making the decision to venture inward and claim your dreams takes courage. (The word *courage* shares a root with the French word *coeur*, meaning "heart.") The first step is to acknowledge that the fears are real and you are strong. In the words of Robert Frost, "The best way out is always through." Or, as I scrawl across the page beneath the poems turned in by students like Deshawn, *Brave work! Keep writing.*

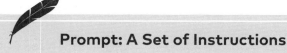

In the poem "Instructions," poet Edward Vidaurre engages a whimsical counting exercise as an antidote to those long hours lying in bed awake. The poem begins: "Cortázar gave me instructions / on how to beat insomnia, on the first night / read to the moon . . ." From there the poem counts down through a series of people and objects (a stranger, a doll, a painting, a book . . .) that the insomniac should address, until it lands on the compelling last line. (No spoilers here, you can read the poem, and enjoy the surprise, online or in Vidaurre's collection *JAZzHOUSE*, from Prickly Pear Publishing.)

Calling to mind a visual hodgepodge of imagery, as Vidaurre does in his poem, is an effective mental activity to induce sleep. That's because the juxtaposition of seemingly random people and things mimics the random neuronal firings of the dreaming mind that may gather into a single dream: your present-day boss, your childhood best friend, and a mama bear lurking beneath the workbench in the garage. Not to mention the fact that Vidaurre's poem ultimately hints at the types of unfinished business that might leave us blocked . . . from sleep or creativity.

Now it's your turn: What instructions would you offer for beating insomnia or writer's block? Are the two connected for you? Can you offer a remedy in the form of a poem or story?

Be submissive to everything, open, listening
No fear or shame in the dignity of your
experience, language, knowledge
Be in love with your life.

—Jack Kerouac, novelist and poet

Goodnight, Censor

Anne Lamott, in her classic handbook for writers, *Bird by Bird*, describes how a hypnotherapist helped her bust through writer's block by transforming the negative voices in her head into imaginary mice. She would pick each one up by the tail, drop it into a jar, fasten the lid, and free herself to write. Despite the playfulness of the technique, she understood that the inner critic is no mere cartoon meanie—its effect is real and it can stop you cold. But there are two sides to this opinionated inner voice and it's worth developing a healthy relationship with it. We can't let it bully us, but we can appreciate the critic's discerning eye when it petitions for adherence to quality standards, or when it holds us back from wantonly acting out unchecked impulses. In other words, when it's time to edit, welcome the critic in—briefly, and with clearly defined tasks to perform. Then encourage it to sit on the sidelines and quiet down while you are generating new material.

The first step is to get to know her or him. For starters, your critic has a known address. It resides in your prefrontal cortex, in a part of your brain that dozes when you dream. And it has a work schedule. Our brain's internal censor (which is perhaps the midnight guise of our daytime critic) is off-duty at night, which is when your dreams come alive with unbridled imagination. This helps explain those racy dreams that make you blush in the morning or make you feel ashamed that you would do something so brazen (even if just in a dream) or that goes against the values you live by in the light of day.

In his book *Imagine*, Jonah Lehrer writes, "Once we fall asleep, the prefrontal cortex shuts itself down; the censor goes eerily quiet." And so during REM sleep, dreaming can accomplish what the day-shift brain (or writing coach) cannot. Some writers take advantage of this knowledge and practice dream incubation and lucid dreaming to clear creative blocks and solve problems of plot and character while they sleep.

In essence, the Dreaming on the Page approach is its own defense against writer's block. By becoming familiar with the sleep and wake cycles of the brain, and by working with dreams and expressing ourselves through writing, we become conscious of the darkness and learn to navigate it. Understanding that dreams provide original and authentic material for poems and stories, and honoring their narrative gifts by journaling them, results in a steady flow of inspiration.

Prompt: Hand the Critic the Mic

When dealing with your inner critic you can befriend them or give them the boot. In this prompt, you'll dress them up as a full-fledged character, hand them a microphone, and turn up the volume. First, what would they wear? How would they move? Where do they spend their time? Now listen in. What do they have to say to you? What might you say in response? Once the critic is out of your head, you'll feel more empowered to write!

You can even do this exercise for five minutes before each writing session. Alternatively, the critic's rants might find their way into a poem or story. Either way, now *you're* in charge!

> *Everything seemed to connect up, the*
> *whole worked well together, and one had*
> *the impression that the Thing was now really*
> *a machine and would soon go by itself.*

—Sigmund Freud, letter to Wilhelm Fliess

Freud or Jung? Associate and Amplify to Find Your Content

Both grandfathers of modern dreamwork, Sigmund Freud and Carl Jung, wove the invisible cords of personal narrative, dream, and transformation into their work.

Freud, a scientist first, wrote in an early letter to his fiancée, Martha Bernays, that his love of books was competing with his fascination with brain anatomy. In particular, Cervantes's *The Colloquy of the Dogs*, which he read as a teenager, is said to have inspired the ideas that would become the basis for Freudian analysis. Freud's *The Interpretation of Dreams* is filled with literary references—most famously the term for one of his signature theories, the Oedipal complex.

Freudian analysis, after all, was in its day a groundbreaking form of therapy that used personal narrative (storytelling) as a psychoanalytic tool. Jung, Freud's protégé-turned-rival, brought ancient stories, in the form of archetype and myth, into the process. Just as literature informed their analytic orientation, both men's influence on literature persists to this day in fields like narrative psychology, in which stories and storytelling are used for therapeutic benefit, and psychoanalytic literary criticism, a broad field that plumbs the interconnections between literature and the psyche.

A dream alone is not literature, and a single work of literature doesn't necessarily pack the personal power of a dream, but the two are closely linked. We will draw on Freudian and Jungian techniques such as free association and amplification and connect the two.

Freud used free association in psychoanalysis to elicit a spontaneous flow of imagery, words, and stories related to a given subject to reveal a patient's underlying issues. In Jungian amplification, the analyst draws on universal stories and myth to elucidate dream material and facilitate psychological healing. Now let's see how both can serve our writing.

Writing Off Freud

Because he reduced dream imagery to sexual terms so freely (interpreting anything from a staircase to a balloon, a train, flower, or skyscraper as representative of genitalia, for example), Freud's legacy is often reduced to a punchline. But we lose out when we overlook his groundbreaking contributions to dream analysis and literature.

Among other things, Freud revolutionized the study of dreams by seeking a scientific explanation for their production and for their relationship to daytime thoughts. Previously, dreams had been relegated to the realm of superstition, divination, and religion. Most important for our purposes is how Freud's study of dreams and psychoanalysis relates to writing. For example:

> **It's all about the id**. Freud's largely debunked theory that dreams primarily represent the fulfillment of repressed desires came in part from his belief that the dreaming mind could slip past the internal censor. He got part of that right. With brain imaging technology (which arrived too late for Freud), scientists have confirmed that parts of the prefrontal cortex that act as gatekeeper for unwanted thoughts and impulses are deactivated during REM sleep. Because the internal censor is quieted during sleep, dreams are

uninhibited by our habitual judgments and personal encyclopedia of taboos, making them valuable for writers and psychotherapists alike.

Play with words. Freud was known to perform near-Talmudic analyses of words when he interpreted a dream, examining each syllable at times and delving into etymology for insight. He pointed out that dreams are masters of wordplay, including puns, verbal slips, neologisms, clever homonyms, and homophones. He treated words themselves as being worthy of analyses, along with any other symbol in a dream. It is in large part thanks to him that we continue to investigate puns and wordplay in dreamwork today.

Talk about yourself. Freud both pioneered the use of inner monologue as a therapeutic device and influenced its use as a literary device. In 1900, the same year *The Interpretation of Dreams* was published, his colleague Arthur Schnitzler, a novelist and a doctor with a passion for psychology, employed interior monologue as an innovative (for the times) technique in his novella *Lieutenant Gustl.* In *The Age of Insight,* author Eric Kandel writes of Schnitzler, "He realized that in taking a patient's medical history, the physician is writing a narrative, one that depends both on the patient's story and on how the physician interprets it." Both Freud and Schnitzler, along with many of their contemporaries, recognized the "literary power of clinical case studies."

Associate freely. Freud may have lifted the idea of using free association in psychoanalysis from an essay on the craft of writing.[6] Either way, the process that analysts continue to use today to elicit memories and stories from their clients is also productive for writers. Free association involves responding to a word or phrase with a stream-of-consciousness cascade of memories and stories. Brainstorming is one form of free association. It is also the basis for free writing, an uncensored style of journaling or writing first drafts.

Prompt: Free to Associate

Get it down. Take chances. It may be bad, but
it's the only way you can do anything really good.

—William Faulkner, Nobel Prize laureate

You can use free association to explore an image from a dream
or a character or place you plan to write about. Then you can use
free writing to start a poem or story. Here's how:

1. Choose a character or image from a dream or from a poem
    or novel you're working on.
2. To connect with your dreamy powers of association, settle
    into your chair and take three to five slow breaths, drawing
    deeper inside yourself on each inhalation, and letting go
    of any resistance or tension, physical or otherwise, on the
    exhalation. Relax your tongue, jaw, and lips to quickly set-
    tle your thoughts.
3. When you're ready, list everything you can about your
    topic. Aim for least twenty associations. Go with the first
    thoughts that come to mind. Here's an example:

    My Grandma Fran: A cigarette balanced in the V of her
    fingers, elegant, distant. In her lounge chair on the patio,
    when I was four years old, pedaling my tricycle round and
    round as she and my mother chatted in the sun. Sunday
    dinners. The green sequined shift hanging in her closet.
    The mothball, smoke, and dusty wood smell of her closet.
    The tickle of the hems of her dresses against my skin as I
    crawled in among them . . .

4. Review your list of associations. What story do these words,
    thoughts, and memories tell? Could the list itself be the
    start of a poem?

5. Set a timer for twelve to twenty minutes and use free writing as you incorporate some or all of your associations into a poem or story. Keep your hand moving as you quickly transcribe your thoughts to the page, without concern for spelling, grammar, or correctness.

Prompt: Amplify by Asking Questions

Write what you hear. Listen to what you write.
Be ready to ask the Proprioceptive Question.

—Linda Trichter Metcalf, PhD, and Tobin Simon, PhD,
Writing the Mind Alive: The Proprioceptive Method for Finding Your Authentic Voice

Whereas Freudian-style free association can help you cover a lot of ground as you give the mind free rein to wander in all directions, Jungian amplification sends you circling down into imagery as you unearth your personal stories as well as collective myths that are evoked by a topic.

The Proprioceptive Question, *What do I mean by* _____ *?*, can be used to amplify a topic.

This question is one of the mainstays in the Proprioceptive Writing (PW) method, a meditative form of process writing developed by Linda Trichter Metcalf, PhD, and Tobin Simon, PhD. In this case, proprioception, from the Latin root *propius* meaning "self," refers to a writing practice designed to explore one's thoughts, emotions, and beliefs. PW employs three simple directions: *Write what you hear. Listen to what you write. Be ready to ask the Proprioceptive Question: What do I mean by* _____ *?* We can use this Proprioceptive Question to investigate a word or phrase in our writing or from a dream. Here's how:

1. For this exercise, write by hand. This will help you slow down and experience the tactile sensations of writing on paper.
2. Take a few breaths. Then start writing by following the first thought that comes to mind. Or you can begin to write a dream—again, starting with whichever scene or image comes to mind first.

3. Unlike in free association, where you write as quickly as you can, this time go at a pace that allows you to "listen to yourself think" and engage with what you're saying on the page.
4. When you come to a word or phrase that pulsates with emotion or energy, pause and write out the question *What do I mean by* _____ ? Fill in the blank with the word or phrase that drew your attention.
5. Then pay attention to the response, which might come in the form of a thought, a memory, or a story.
6. Keep writing and ask the question *What do I mean by* _____ ? as often as needed.
7. Notice how the Proprioceptive Question acts as a headlamp, shining a beam of light into the word or concept you are exploring to reveal unexpected pathways to follow.

Dream is the personalized myth,
myth the depersonalized dream.

—Joseph Campbell, writer

Make It Mythic

Maybe your relationship to your father was like that of Regan to King Lear, or you are raising a teen girl and are drawn to the story of Demeter and Persephone. Okay, both of those examples relate to me, and writing poems in which I reimagined each of these myths (collective dreams) helped me identify and heal issues and patterns in my life.

More recently, I dreamed about characters from a classic television show, *The Gilmore Girls*. The relationship between the main characters, a teenage girl coming of age and her unconventional single mother, resonated with me both as a daughter and as a mom. I worked on the dream using amplification and realized that these fictional characters were helping me explore my own experiences as an unconventional mother and as the daughter of a mother who was a nonconformist and an iconoclast.

What myths from ancient literature or contemporary culture resonate with your dreams and stories?

Mythic dreams. Do any of your dreams follow a version of the hero's (or heroine's) journey? Might a dream of being lost resonate with Homer's *Odyssey*? What about that Oz-like dream of wandering through a fantastical landscape that helped you understand your real-life journey better?
Under review. Now look at the poems and stories you are writing. Are there echoes of a particular mythic tale there? (The word *echo*, by the way, comes from a character in Greek mythology. Once you start to look, you'll see that mythic references are everywhere!)

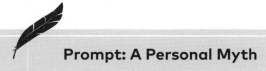

Prompt: A Personal Myth

Write your life story as if it were a fairy tale, using these sentence starters to guide you:

> *This is the story of a child who . . .*
> *Every day . . .*
> *Then one day . . .*
> *Because of that . . .*
> *And finally . . .*

> *The work of condensation in dreams is seen at its clearest when it handles words and names.*
>
> —Sigmund Freud, *The Interpretation of Dreams*

The Art of Condensation

It's unusual to be able to print a memoir on a single page. But I wrote a story that spanned more than three decades of my life that could have fit onto a postcard. An image from a dream helped me sink straight into the heart of the story so I could encapsulate a family saga in so small a space.

As Freud said, dreams, with their knack for taking an epic tale and boiling it down to its essence, are masters at condensation. I think that's what happened when I wrote "Our Return to Tenderness," the story of my relationship with my daughter, in under a hundred words. Although the dream isn't explicitly referenced in this flash memoir, which was published in the *New York Times* Tiny Love Stories column and anthology, it was inspired by a dream fragment that is described in the last four sentences.

Our Return to Tenderness

I used to lift you overhead, laughter reverberating from your infant throat. "You're going to be a party girl," I cooed. Your childhood was no party though. Custody battles. Your other mother won. At age 10, you were returned to me. During your teen years, that party girl let loose. Defiance, slammed doors, a DUI. Finally, you asked for help. "My baby's inside there," I said, pointing to your heart. "Take care of her." Five months sober now, you say, "Show me how." Once, you had no patience for tender words. Today you drink them in.[7]

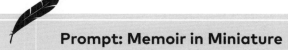

Prompt: Memoir in Miniature

Bring to mind a dream about someone you love. Focus on one image or moment from the dream (or from life) and boil down this chronicle of closeness and conflict into a miniature story or essay of one hundred words, or fewer if you can.

Prompt: The Art of Erasure

Dreams often go for baroque. They pile on high-decibel emotions, evocative images, colorful characters, and soap opera–worthy plot twists, until it can all feel like too much! To pare back that ornately rendered experience and connect with its essence, try writing an erasure poem. I live in New England, so the process of making rich, dark maple syrup from a tasteless, colorless sap comes to mind when I want to describe how to write an erasure poem. To make one gallon of maple syrup, you'd boil about forty gallons of sap. Over the course of many hours, anything that's not sweet and dark goes up in smoke. Similarly, in an erasure poem we lift out any words that are flat, weak, and bland and extract what's sweet, rich, and delicious.

For inspiration, look at Lucille Clifton's sparse poems "my dream about time," "my dream about the cows," or "my dream about being white," which can be found in her book *Blessing the Boats* and online. Then write an erasure poem using a dream as a text to achieve the benefits of condensation. Here's how:

1. Choose a recent dream or recurring dream to work with.
2. Write the dream down. Include details and description.
3. Replace any vague or weak words with words that help you see, hear, or feel the image or action more clearly.
4. Strike out phrases that are overly wordy, redundant, or unnecessary. Strike phrases that are abstract or vague.
5. Create a line break between each action in the poem—or wherever you feel a visual or sonic pause is needed.
6. Give your creation a title. You might even pay homage to Clifton by titling your poem "My Dream About . . ."
7. Review your poem, letting your intuition lead the way. Can you cut even more?
8. Presto: You've created a dream erasure poem!

The images in dreams
are images I can trust.

—Pat Fargnoli, poet

Imagery: The Stuff of Dreams

Dream images are supernovas pulsating with energy and packed with the potential to illuminate your inner life. No mere illustrations, they are shimmering calls for connection and confrontation and provide portals into realms of insight, information, and meaning.

Austrian American psychoanalyst Ernest Hartmann taught that meaningful and memorable dreams contain a central image that catches your attention and holds the key to identifying the dream's underlying emotion. But even the imagery in ordinary dreams is worth exploring, according to Jung. Each object, from a book on the shelf in the background of the dream living room to the clouds in the dream sky, carries energy and meaning that can reveal truths about our lives.

Poets understand the elemental tension that makes an image vibrate with aliveness. In her book *What It Is*, cartoonist and author Lynda Barry explains her take on the image like this: "It's not alive in the way you and I are alive, but it's certainly not dead. It's alive in the way our memory is alive. Alive in the way the ocean is alive and able to transport us and contain us."

To wake up the imagery from dreams and imagination, we go beyond describing them and enter a relationship with those seemingly inanimate objects. Speaking of artists and their imagery, Jung wrote, "Face the figures of the vision actively and reactively, with full consciousness." Transformation, he taught, occurs when we eschew interpretation of images and instead engage with them. This is potent guidance for dreamers and writers.

Prompt: Activate Your Imagination

When the image speaks, it is with one of our own inner voices.

—Robert A. Johnson, *Inner Work*

Active imagination, a form of dreaming while you are awake, allows you to have an enlivened dialogue with dream images. Here's how:

1. Get centered. Take a few breaths, and as you let go with each exhalation, allow yourself to get still, then quiet, then open and expansive.
2. Focus on an image from a dream. Take your time to see it clearly and experience it with all of your senses.
3. Get curious about this image and notice what's around it. Is there anything or anyone else present?
4. Insert yourself as a character into the story. Notice where you are in relation to the image or object. What's around you? How old are you?
5. Ask questions of this image or object and listen for answers.
6. Write a poem or story based on this inner journey, beginning with the words *I am*. Then write directly from the perspective of the image.

In the next exercise, you can take this exploration a step further.

Voices in the Night

In literature—especially children's literature—teacups and tableware have personalities and a fondness for singing and dancing. When I was a child, my house and the fixtures and furniture in it were alive for me, too. The S-pipe beneath the sink in the half bath in the downstairs hallway was a long-faced elder with a wise and comforting presence. The blue wingback armchair by the living room window was a friendly maternal companion who held me in her lap while I paged through my chapter books. As a teenager, I would no longer have admitted this secret even to myself, but when the house was sold and we moved away, I grieved as if I were leaving behind a beloved aunt or uncle. I now understand that animating nature, houses, and furniture isn't child's play—nor is it childish—except in the sense that children are sensitive to the power of imagination and they still sense the aliveness of the world.

In dreamwork we give voice to objects from our reveries. In writing we render objects with care and precision. Animating what is inanimate can help us connect with our surroundings and bring more music and magic to the mundane and our writing.

Prompt: The World of Objects

It is well, at certain hours of the day and night, to look closely at the world of objects at rest. . . . The used surfaces of things, the wear that the hands give to things, the air, tragic at times, pathetic at others, of such things—all lend a curious attractiveness to the reality of the world that should not be underprized.

—Pablo Neruda, "Toward an Impure Poetry"

Choose an image from a dream, or from a poem or story you are working on. (Or you can use the same one you used in the previous exercise.)

1. Get centered again.
2. Take a few minutes with your eyes closed to observe everything about that image: its size, its shape, its weight, any colors that you see. Get close enough to smell it. What would it taste like? Experience this object with all of your senses. Then pretend that you *are* this object.
3. Respond to the following questions. Don't overthink this; go with your first thought each time:

   I am a:
   My purpose is:
   What I like best is:
   What I dislike most is:
   What I fear most is:
   What I desire most is:
   I have come to tell you:

4. Reread what you've written. Lightly edit, and see if you can find a poem, story, or the seed for another creative expression within it.[8]

PRO TIP: WRITE WITH THE "WRONG" HAND

When doing this exercise, try writing the questions with your dominant hand (your right hand if you are right-handed, or your left hand if you are left-handed), and let the object answer while writing with your pen in the other hand. Doing this helps you activate your unconscious mind and get in touch with your dreamy imagination quickly and easily. You may also want to try this technique (writing with the "other" hand) when working with other prompts, or when investigating the messages in your dreams in general.

But poetry—which awakens our senses, frees us from the tyranny of literal meaning and assures us of the credible reality of emotional truth—puts us in touch with something bigger than language . . .

—Tracy K. Smith, from her remarks at the Library of Congress

Five Open Doors

Our five senses can act as portals into that the present moment, that postage stamp–sized patch of terrain we habitually stumble past, barely noticing it at all. The easiest way to find joy in the moments of your day is to tune into taste, touch, sight, sound, and smell with lucid awareness. In the space of a minute, you will have become a little clearer and calmer—and a little more in love with your everyday existence. As writers, we especially need that nudge into presence that the senses can provide. Again, our dreams can help.

When we dream, our physical senses are muted, which helps us stay in a state of slumber undistracted by the scent of fumes from a passing car outside the open window, or the ticking of the clock, or the slide of sheets on skin. But when our eyes close, our inner vision opens up. The secondary visual cortex, which lets us see clearly in our dreams, is activated in REM sleep. Sometimes, in fact, our sense of sight is heightened to a Technicolor precision beyond what our eyes can see when awake. The other four senses are submerged into dullness for most people, so we are less likely to recall sounds, smells, tastes, and tactile sensations from dreams when we wake up—but they are there, too.

To restore the full range of sensory experience of dreams, write the absent senses back into your dream report in your journal. As you write, imagine your way back into the dream and ask yourself: "If this were happening now, what else might I see? Smell? Taste? Touch? Hear?" Doing this will enliven your experience of the dream in hindsight. You may also begin to experience more sense stimuli in future dreams, including hearing music, experiencing highly sensitized touch, or getting an occasional whiff or taste of a dreamy meal.

Prompt: Open All the Doors

Until now, you've most likely relied heavily on the sense of sight when writing about your dreams. Generally speaking, it's not unusual for writers to rely primarily on visual details. Try these prompts to help restore the other four senses:

Compensation. Write about a dream, poem, or story without using the sense of sight. Notice what other powers of observation you call forth and which other senses are heightened when you stop relying on descriptions of what you see.

Walk in silence. Take a silent, solo walk for twenty minutes or more. Leave your headphones and earbuds at home. Don't talk to anyone or squander your attention on your phone. Quiet any distracting thoughts by bringing your focus to your five senses. Then sit down and write about what you experienced.

"It would sound like a dream," said Billy.

—Kurt Vonnegut, *Slaughterhouse-Five*

The Sounds of Sleeping

My husband tells me I'm a loud sleeper. "Lord save us," I mutter in the night, then snuggle my cheek deeper into my pillow and snore. Apparently, my repertoire includes talking, sighing, moaning, and occasionally calling out while I snooze.

But behind the curtain of my sleeping mind, it's a quieter story. Tucked into our cottony dreams, we are ensconced within ourselves, even as the world ticks on in the rooms around us. It's like being in a group of people yet feeling cozily alone inside oneself. In this sense, the soundscape of the dream is hushed and insular.

Sure, some nights we hear music or mayhem in our dreams. Occasionally the voice of timeless wisdom booms forth from within, too. But for most of us, most nights, our dreams are muted, as though they're tiptoeing through the night, so as not to wake the dreamer.

Prompt: With an Ear to the Dream

Now, put your ear against your dream and tune in. With a lock-smith's attention, listen for the quietest sound. Try to hear the delicate pings of small tumblers turning to unlock the treasures and secrets within. Here are some exercises to help amplify the sounds of dreaming:

1. Choose a dream that had a distinctive sound to work with, or for an extra challenge, choose a dream that seems silent to you, and fill in the sounds.
2. What sounds do you remember in the dream? If you don't remember any sounds from the dream, imagine what sounds might have been present in this scenario.
3. Now, write a poem or paragraph using these sentence starters:

   This dream sounds like . . .
   In this dream, I hear . . .

4. Or write a poem or story based on your dream, paying special attention to the sounds.

   You can modify these instructions to tune into any of the other senses as well.

WRITING
THE
SELF

The wind is ghosting around the house tonight
and as I lean against the door of sleep
I begin to think about the first person to dream . . .

—Billy Collins, "The First Dream"

Autobiography in Dreams

In the first dream I remember, I am four years old, standing barefoot in my nightgown at the top of the stairs. Peering down, with my nose pressed between the spindles of the railing, it's as if I've lifted the roof of a dollhouse to reveal the honeycombed rooms inside. Below me, I see my father, caught unaware, seated cross-legged on the living room floor. He has shed his jacket but still wears the button-down shirt he'd have worn to work that day, whose detergent and sweat-spiced scent I knew from when my cheek cradled against it as he carried me up to bed after I'd fallen asleep in front of the TV. "Sleep tight. Don't let the bed bugs bite," he'd say. And then flick off the light.

But in the dream, he's not comforting me. He's holding up a Mickey Mouse doll—only to break it open. An army of little mice escapes from inside of it and fan out through the house to attack. It was a scene like the one I'd seen in *Fantasia* earlier that night on TV. It would have been scary enough to frighten me awake, but I must not have cried out, because if I had, my sister would have woken up, and my mother would have swept into my room in her long green robe and shushed me back to sleep. "It's only a dream," she would have said.

It's the first dream I remember telling anyone. My first audience was my big sister, who slept in her twin bed just a few steps away from mine. My parents, hearing the account in the sunlit kitchen over slices of toast, laughed. "What an imagination on that one," my dad would say.

That autumn, I pedaled my pink Schwinn behind the moving van along with my sister and brother. We were moving into a new, bigger house, just a few blocks away. For the first time, I had my own bedroom. It was unsettling sleeping by myself in that big room. But my dreams had come with me, so I wasn't ever all alone. My father moved out a few years later, and my parents' divorce seemed like the very worst thing that could happen.

I like to think that my first dream helped me prepare for everything that was to come after—all the big and small fears that swarmed out of that nightmare, out of those early years. It was then that I learned that wherever I moved, and whatever "worst thing" happened along the way, my dreams would come with me—and teach me to be brave.

Prompt: Tell Your Sleep Story

Bedtime doesn't have one singular cozy connotation for me. As a child, I feared the dark and simultaneously loved my dreams. And even that love was complex, as I had disturbing dreams as often as I had wonderful ones. Then, as an adult, sleep and dreams became a source of study as well as a font of spiritual and emotional support. Maybe that's why I long for the simple yearning in Meredith Holmes's poem "In Praise of Bed." The poem begins:

> At last I can be with you!
> The grinding hours
> since I left your side!

and ends with these lines:

> I close my eyes, hear myself
> moan, so grateful to be held this way.

Now it's your turn. Settle in—under the covers if you like—and write your own bedtime ode. Let your ode be a poem of praise, but don't shy away from nuance or complicated truths, either. Describe in your own way the yearning, the longing, the falling into and the being in your bed! Following Holmes's example, write directly to your bed using the second person pronoun (*you*), which will add intimacy to your words.

Prompt: Reading Dreams

We are all trapped in stories . . . each of us a prisoner of our own solipsistic narrative, each family the captive of the family story, each community locked within its own tale of itself, each people the victims of their own versions of history.

—Salman Rushdie, *Two Years Eight Months and Twenty-Eight Nights*

It's hard to take in the scope of a story that is as close, and large, as the story of your own life. To get perspective, pick up one of your journals as if it were a book you plucked at random from a shelf in your local library or favorite bookstore, and let your dreams have their say. Page through and read each dream as if it's a chapter in this saga. Just as when you pick up a brand-new book by an unknown author, keep an open mind, get curious, and ask questions:

1. Who is the protagonist in this story? What other characters play important roles?
2. What does the protagonist know? What do others seem to know about this character that she or he doesn't know?
3. What might the author be trying to tell the reader?
4. Now write the story these dreams seem to be telling about your life. Start with the words *In this story* and keep writing. To make it a poem, you might begin each line (or every few lines) with that phrase.

WRITING THE OTHER: CHARACTERS, CREATURES, AND CRITTERS

> *I actually see myself in all my characters.*
> *In order to imagine what it feels like to be*
> *another person I have to use my own*
> *experiences and responses to the world.*
>
> —Elizabeth Strout, author of *Olive Kitteridge*

Building Character

Most nights, you play the starring role in your dreams. You embark on journeys, fight off attackers, and dine with friends in foreign cities. The narratives that unfold are presented from the perspective of what a dream analyst would call the dream ego (the representation of the dreamer in the dream) and what in literature we'd call the protagonist (the main character). The dream story typically revolves around our actions as we find our way out of fixes or into the arms of amorous lovers, but the plot is propelled forward by a full cast of characters, some known to us and some unknown.

This army of begrudging, badgering, bossy, bemused, or beneficent "others" pushes the dream drama in new directions and adds interest and intrigue to the action. We can bring these characters to the page to inhabit our poems and stories. Writing about them can also help us get to know ourselves better.

A foundational belief in many approaches to dreamwork is that every character in a dream is expressing a part of ourselves. This isn't always a comfortable concept to embrace, especially when characters in our dream act up or act out in ways we don't like or agree with. But the more we can recognize and accept the complications and contradictions in our own character, the better equipped we are to create compelling characters on the page. For now, go on faith that all dreams come in the service of health, help, and healing, and allow yourself to entertain the possibility that getting to know the full cast of characters living inside you will help you evolve into the best version of yourself possible.

Prompt: Minor Characters

Examine the role (pun unavoidable) that the so-called minor characters play in your dreams. These are the unknown extras who usually get short shrift in both dreamwork and writing. Follow these steps to get started:

1. Choose a character from a dream, preferably someone you don't know in your waking life. Write down the character's name (if you know it) or any identifying label, such as *Cook, Teacher*, or *Woman in Blue Dress*.
2. Describe what they are doing, how they move, and what they are saying.
3. List three personality traits or qualities that come to mind when you think of this character. Go with the first three things that come to mind. There are no wrong answers here.
4. Now that you've gotten to know your character, write in the first person, starting with the words *I am . . .* , and tell this character's story.

The Good News About Bad Guys

We lock our doors, screen our phone calls, and spend a good deal of energy avoiding contact with bad guys, both in waking hours and in dreams. And that makes sense; it's important to protect ourselves from people who can't be trusted to treat us well. But dreams and the imagination offer a safe space to take a closer look at people we'd normally keep on the other side of the welcome mat. These might be people who annoy us, threaten, or scare us. And as much as we might want to avoid these folks in waking life, on the page they can be valuable assets. They are the devilish characters who advocate for conflicting points of view. They might add suspense, friction, and variety to spice up a scene. Think about it: There must be a reason that so many actors say that their favorite role was when they stepped into the villain's shoes.

So, keep your boundaries strong, but let yourself explore some bad apples from your dreams on the page.

Prompt: Play the Villain

Writing about villains isn't just a good literary exercise, it also helps us take a constructive look at the parts of our personalities that we try to hide away out of sight. Letting these bad guys have a voice in our writing can be a healthy way to study and understand them—and ultimately ourselves. So, return to one of these prompts above: "Hand the Critic the Mic" (page 98) or "Minor Characters" (page 127). In either case, try the exercise using a disliked or scary character from one of your dreams.

Archetypes: The Original Central Casting

It's as if there's a central casting company in the clouds supplying a steady stream of stock characters to populate our nightly dramas. To see what I mean, flip through the pages of your dream journal. You'll likely find passionate lovers, menacing intruders, sage grandmothers, innocent babies, and maybe even a watchful washerwoman, cantankerous cashier, or homeless vet. A Jungian analyst might connect these characters to the archetypes they represent (and which can be found in most any tarot deck): the Lover, the Devil, the Wise Elder, the Trickster, the Fool, or the Warrior.

The word *archetype* comes from the ancient Greek and refers to the first model of a thing. In *The Collected Works of C. G. Jung,* Robert Hopcke writes, "The archetype is like a psychic mold into which individual and collective experiences are poured and where they take shape." Different cultures may have different names for specific archetypes, but they point toward the same basic characteristics.

Unlike stereotypes, which diminish and mask a person's complexity and uniqueness, an archetype reveals something foundational about who they are. Archetypes can point us toward the potential that lies within our cranky uncle, for example—as well as how people's challenges and shortcomings may mute or distort that potential.

Once you have an eye out for them, you'll find archetypes throughout literature and popular culture. We find the Fool in Shakespeare's comedies, echoes of the Wise Elder in Judge Judy, and the Priestess in Oprah. But more than that, we can find all these archetypes within ourselves. We each contain the whole cast of characters, from the Infant, to the Warrior, to the Crone, to the King. Each of these types (and more) appear in our dreams in a variety of costumes, making them sometimes easy and sometimes more difficult to identify.

The subject of archetypes can get complicated. But even a passing familiarity with them can help you think differently about the characters you dream up on the pillow and on the page—not to mention the characters you encounter in your life each day.

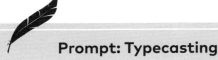

Prompt: Typecasting

Review a selection of dreams from your journal, and begin to identify which archetypes show up there. They may neatly align with the classic archetypes but more likely they will not. Consider each one carefully, then see how many archetypes you can identify:

1. As you search for examples of archetypes in your dreams, stay open to finding your personal variations on them. How about in your writing? Start keeping a list of the archetypes that appear in your essays, stories, and poems. Which make the most frequent appearances?

2. In addition to noting which archetypes recur in your dreams and in your writing, make note of which ones are missing. Are your dreams and drafts filled with Warriors but missing Wise Elders? Lots of Fools and Babies but no nurturing Mothers?

3. Consider what the presence and absence of different archetypes tell you about your strengths on the page and off, and where you might be out of balance. Too many damsels in distress? Maybe you need to invite a heroine to the page.

4. Take an archetypal figure from a dream and introduce that type into something you're writing. Or, intentionally insert one of the missing archetypes into your writing. Notice what happens when you do.

> *When Gregor Samsa woke up one morning*
> *from unsettling dreams, he found himself*
> *changed in his bed into a monstrous vermin.*
>
> —Franz Kafka, *The Metamorphosis*

Metamorphoses (Or, What to Do When You Wake Up as a Bug)

I tell the young moms in my poetry class that we are going to write about cockroaches today. They look from one to the other, exchanging looks that seem to ask, "Is she crazy?"

Not only that, I continue, we're going to read a love poem about a cockroach, and we're going to explore what the cockroach might be feeling. Then we'll write love notes to or from cockroaches, or Dear John letters, or maybe even letters expressing their soul's desires. Now they exchange those *She's not really going to make us do this, is she?* looks. They're teenagers, after all; they have their pride.

We read Martín Espada's poem "My Cockroach Lover," which includes these lines:

> One night I dreamed
> a giant roach
> leaned over me,
> brushing my face
> with kind antennae
> and whispered, "I love you."

When we are done, Sarai blurts out: "That poem is whack! But it's also pretty funny."

After a few minutes we are all sharing experiences of times when our homes were overrun by ladybugs or ants, or cockroaches—and sometimes these insect invaders even crept into our dreams. But Espada took the experience even further. In his poem he let his imagination have free rein, and he brought his dream—and the cockroach—fully alive.

"That's what makes the poem so great," I say. "The poet didn't flinch from the roach."

"Or squash it!" Sarai exclaims.

"Right! Instead, he kept his gaze on the creepy insect and even let himself imagine the possibility of falling in love with it!"

As it turns out, there's a grand tradition of poems about cockroaches. In "The Coming of Archy," by Don Marquis, for example, a cockroach types a soulful letter. After all, stepping into another creature's . . . well . . . not skin exactly, is the magic trick writers perform daily.

Whitman used poetry to slip inside another person's experience in "Song of Myself." He imagined what it would be like to be different races and a different gender. He even wrote of passing "death with the dying, and birth with the new-wash'd babe." That's the shimmering transcendence of art; the leap of imagination from the writer's body into that of the other.

Through the power of the imagination, we can sense what it's like to be someone—or something—else. So much so that we might even find ourselves getting swoony over a bug!

When it was time for my students to write that day, I relented. I told the class they didn't really have to write letters as if they were cockroaches. "You can write from the point of view of an ant, a spider, a ladybug . . . or any creepy-crawly thing."

My students' poems, as usual, were dazzling. Sarai's cockroach wrote a love note that began, "I am the one you've been looking for . . ." By the end we were all smitten—by a bug we would otherwise be more likely to crush beneath our heel.

Prompt: Get Buggy

Write a letter from the point of view of a creepy-crawly or winged insect. Discover what poignant, powerful, or peculiar perspectives these often ignored, despised, or misunderstood creatures have to offer:

- Write about an insect you encountered in waking life or in a dream.
- Include two things the bug is doing, two things it's feeling, two things it fears, and two things it dreams of.
- Write in first person, as if you are the insect, starting each line with statements such as *I am...*, *I feel...*, or *I dream...*

Prompt: Shift Shapes

Shape-shifting isn't as far-out as it seems. Writers do it all the time; we inhabit other bodies to open new possibilities on the page. You can amp up your shape-shifting powers in lucid dreams or in an awakened dream state by shifting your perspective so you experience the world through the eyes of a bobcat, an inchworm, or your pet bunny rabbit. Or use your imagination to transform yourself into the creatures or characters you encounter today. Whichever method you choose, write about it.

WRITING
PLACES

> *If I were asked to name the chief benefit*
> *of the house, I should say: the house shelters*
> *day-dreaming, the house protects the dreamer,*
> *the house allows one to dream in peace.*

—Gaston Bachelard, *The Poetics of Space*

In the House of Dreams

I dream about houses with no walls, and I feel oddly safe and happy as snow drifts into the living room and with nothing keeping traffic noises or passersby out.

I also have recurring dreams about the house I grew up in: an early twentieth-century white stucco house on a corner lot in a middle-class neighborhood on Long Island. But while I dream, obsess, and write about my childhood home, the *idea* of home expands beyond the four walls of any house, real or imagined, contemporary or remembered.

Houses in dreams are said to stand in for the self: windows for eyes, doors representing what you are letting in or locking out, and so on.

The fairy-tale houses of straw, wood, and brick, or the ones made of gingerbread or constructed from an old shoe, shelter our childhood memories. From Nathaniel Hawthorne's *The House of the Seven Gables* to Ann Patchett's *Dutch House* (in which a storied house anchors a family's rise and fall from ostentatious abundance to pitiful deprivation), houses represent the archetypal and elusive dream of home.

The poem "House" by Charles Simic wakes the reader from the illusion that a house is merely a collection of timber and nails or brick and mortar, into the truth of the vibrant aliveness of the places we call home: "My house has grown smaller," he writes. As the poem continues, we discover that this house wears boots, its noises echo loudly, and the legs of the kitchen table dig holes in the earth.

The houses in our dreams are similarly strange and malleable. Seemingly familiar houses sprout new rooms and shed walls. Their doors won't lock. Their staircases refuse to lead us to familiar rooms. And sometimes they glow with unearthly light.

Prompt: Dream House

As you consider the houses in your dreams, unlock all the doors. Peer into all the dark corners, open the closets, and climb into the attic of your dream house. Peek under the bed and discover the secret stories that are sheltered beneath it. Then use these prompts to guide your writing:

> *In this house, I see . . . I hear . . . I smell . . . I touch . . .*
> *In this house, I discover . . .*
> *This house knows . . .*
> *Now it is time to . . .*

Location, Location

In his poem "Kubla Kahn," Samuel Taylor Coleridge transcribed his hallucinatory vision of Xanadu, with its domed skyline and coursing river, to the page. I have never dreamed of Xanadu, but I have dreamed of a world where cheese grows on trees, and of crystalline waters where magnificent creatures swim. Perhaps you, too, have dreamed of lush locales you've never traveled to when awake or fantastical otherworldly landscapes that can't be found on any map.

The landscapes in literature, as in dreams, can transport us far away without ever leaving home. But they do more than just set the scene where the action plays out. The setting tells us where we are located—both literally and metaphorically. If a novel takes place in a library, we can expect a literal or figurative search for knowledge to take place. If the ground beneath our feet is crusted with snow and ice in a dream, we might consider whether we are frozen into grief, despair, or some stuck way of thinking.

The places you dream up reveal where you are in your emotional journey. They can also provide context, lend an air of veracity to a scene, or even provide blueprints for new worlds in science fiction or fantasy stories. Or they can do double duty on the page and also illustrate a character's state of mind.

Prompt: Step into a Dream

In the novel *1984* by George Orwell, dreams and waking inhabit the same plot of land during one memorable scene in which Winston, the main character, studies the landscape:

> Suddenly he was standing on short springy turf, on a summer evening when the slanting rays of the sun gilded the ground. The landscape that he was looking at recurred so often in his dreams that he was never fully certain whether or not he had seen it in the real world.

Spoiler alert: Winston will return to this territory in his waking life.

Later, at the end of the novel, Orwell employs his dreams again for dramatic effect. Take note of the role a dreamscape can play in advancing plot. Also notice the descriptive language Orwell uses in recounting the dream. What do you see in your mind's eye and how do you feel as you read his lines?

Now, inspired by Orwell's writing, use these prompts to write about a dream location:

1. Describe a location from a dream in detail. What kind of place is it? What are the distinguishing features of this place? Are there steep cliffs? An inviting park? Paved lots or gently rolling hills? Is it deserted or densely inhabited?
2. Place a character in this setting and see what happens. You might start with the phrase *In this place . . .*
3. Inspired by Orwell's writing, try these sentence starters, too:

   Suddenly I was standing in . . .
   This landscape recurred again and again in dreams . . .
   I call it . . .
   But in waking life . . .

WRITING
PLOT

I worship at the altar of intention and obstacle. Somebody wants something, and something is standing in their way of getting it.

—Aaron Sorkin, in an interview in the *New York Times Magazine*, March 8, 2020

A Productive Collision

As a teenager, when I came to my mother with my tattered heart in my hands after a cute boy at school broke up with me, she would look up from the book she was reading and say, "You'll get a good story out of this." I was looking for a reassuring hug and consoling words—and maybe a plate of fresh-baked cookies straight from the oven. But that wasn't the mother I got. And while her response stoked my adolescent angst, as I got older I appreciated her "turn lemons into literature" philosophy. She was right, after all. The mythical easy life has its appeal, but no one is going to read a book about it.

A juicy plot, as any writing teacher (or, in my case anyway, tough-love mother) will tell you, is what happens when the protagonist's will and her destiny collide. Destiny, it turns out, is almost always something the character does *not* want. Think *Gilgamesh*. Okay, that's ancient history—literally. Think about the last novel you read. Think about yourself when you were sixteen and were sure you'd met The One, only to discover that to them you were just one among many. Plot happens when someone thinks she knows where her life is headed and then . . . enter the pink slip, the diagnosis, the unexpected positive pregnancy test.

The hero's journey, plotted out by Joseph Campbell, begins with the hero in his (we'll stick with the masculine pronoun here, as Campbell specifically addressed the male—and not the female—heroic journey) familiar habitat, until he receives a call to adventure. Were he to accept at that early stage, books would be a lot shorter—and less interesting (less relatable, too). Because what makes the journey heroic is that the task is bigger than he is, and he refuses the call, until he's pushed and pushed and, finally, he accepts.

Yes, it's a lot of fuss. But the plot would never thicken, and the hero would remain no more interesting than a nice guy from Spokane, if he received the call and picked up on the first ring.

Similarly, dreams tap at the door until we open it and confront whoever is there. They insist that we step outside and follow our destiny's shimmering story line. Most of the time, however, we turn over, hit snooze, and refuse to wake up to our soul's true calling.

For the adventure-averse, or the writer whose story is bloated with description and in need of a plot point to spice things up, dreams with their blanket-wringing twists and turns make for ideal coaches. They'll nudge and prod, but they'll never push you past where you have the potential to go.

If you really want to uncover the lesson of a dream, identify and study the point of conflict. That's the plot of ground, so to speak, where the action gets interesting. Consider the obstacles and dangers of a dream as signposts that a plot turn is about to lead you into the heart of whatever issues you are dealing with. These moments are usually marked in dream reports by words like *suddenly* or *out of the blue* or even an innocuous-seeming *and then*. These are the syllables on which plots turn. Once you start looking, you'll see that your dreams are rife with them: You are driving your dream car home through spring-green fields, and *suddenly* the road is flooded and you can't go any farther. You're bobbing on the sea in a boat, when *suddenly* a fin slices the water and you realize you're holding an umbrella instead of a paddle. You're walking down a country lane at dusk, and *out of the blue* a bear appears.

These plot thickeners don't just make for a good story—they are testing grounds for our protagonists—and for ourselves as we experience our dream adventures. As writers and dreamers, we imagine our way out of various corners and feel along the walls till we find the hidden door where we can exit what seemed otherwise like a dead end. In our search for meaningful and satisfying conclusions, we need to (figuratively at least) get our boots muddy and maybe even slay—or better yet befriend—a dragon or two. After all, conflict is an unavoidable part of life. What's most important is how we use it to learn and grow.

In dreams, clashes, discord, and points of friction can help prepare us for challenges we might face when we're awake. Science has shown that rehearsing possible reactions to stressful or threatening situations is one function of dreams. Reading and writing stories, like dreaming, allows us to slip into different destinies, discover our powers, summon our strength—and make better informed choices when we open our eyes or close the book.

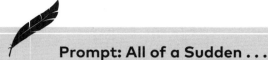

Prompt: All of a Sudden . . .

Page through your dream reports and underline words and phrases like *and then*, *suddenly*, and *out of the blue*. These words signal that the plot is about to take a turn. Notice what happens just before those words appear and what happens after. You'll start to see that when you become afraid in a dream, what happens next will be scary: the cat begins to hiss, the baby falls from your arms, or an ocean tide begins to tug you under. When you realize you need help, "suddenly there was a hospital in sight" or, as happens often in dreams, "I tried to call for help, but my phone wouldn't work." Your beliefs or expectations can trigger a new twist: "I was handed a colorful ticket that I hadn't purchased and I felt sad because . . ." And that's when the dreamscape changes from a cotton candy–sweet carnival to a deserted field. What might have been different if that unexpected ticket had elicited excitement instead?

With this in mind, begin to write a story or poem. After two or three sentences, drop an *and suddenly* into the action. For example, *and suddenly*—

> *the brakes stopped working*
> *a stranger tapped him on the shoulder*
> *she noticed an unusual animal coming toward her*
> *the phone rang*
> *a shadowy figure approached the house*

Then, watch what happens.

Prompt: A Stranger Comes to Town

It's one of the oldest plot devices there is: *a stranger comes to town . . .* In our dreams the stranger may show up as someone whose face we know as well as our own but who appears in strange garments (the father who was never a soldier in full uniform). Or we may encounter total strangers, nameless others, who push the story into new territory.

Look through your dreams to find an example of a character coming toward you, whose appearance on the scene sets the narrative in motion or pushes it into a new direction. Use these prompts to keep the story going:

> *I see _____ coming toward me . . .*
> *I notice _____*
> *S/he has stories to tell about _____*
> *S/he has changed this story by _____*

Now that you've written the stranger alive, keep writing!

WRITING
THROUGH
DARKNESS

We sleep and are awake
We dream and are not here;
Our spirits walk elsewhere
With shadow folk.

—Hilda Doolittle, "Projector"

Invite Your Shadow in for Tea

A slithering tendril of knife-cold air wrapped itself around my neck. I looked around the white-tiled room but no one was there. Still, the danger was palpable and a shiver crept across my skin. I called to my husband for help. Silence. And then, a voice at my back answered: "No one is coming to help you."

My spine stiffened and my knees turned to ice. *This is a nightmare*, I thought.

A nightmare! This realization woke me up within the dream. Lucid now, I remembered: I know how to deal with scary dreams. So, I gathered my courage and swiveled around to face the direction the voice had come from. But there was no one there. Just a curtained window. I yanked open the heavy fabric to reveal . . . a frog hunched on the sill.

"You?" I asked, incredulous that this comical green lump had summoned all that terror in me. "Why are you doing this to me?"

"Don't you like to talk about these things with your students?" the frog asked.

"If by 'these things,' you mean nightmares, yes."

This insouciant amphibian went on to explain that he was doing me a favor by handing me more material for my work. The nightmare mood dissolved into comedy and I woke smiling.

My visitor was right. Whenever someone tells me a nightmare, I sit up a little straighter in my chair and lean in toward them. "I know it sounds crazy," I say, "but I love to work with nightmares." I proceed to tell them how nightmares led me on my healing path and inspired me to want to work with others and their dreams.

Nightmares also fill my poems: the cat's grave, the drowned girl, footsteps approaching in the night. A friend once remarked after reading my poetry, "You seem like such a happy person, I had no idea you had this dark side, too." I explained that I'm happy *because* I have creative outlets for my anxieties and fears.

No one looks forward to scary dreams. But shutting them out shuts off a valuable source of wisdom, not to mention a source of inspiration. Mary Shelley's *Frankenstein* came from a dream, as did Stephenie Meyer's *Twilight* novels.

In dreamwork we investigate the dark corners of our consciousness and learn to confront the worm-cold memories and stinging truths that we might otherwise resist facing. Jung said, "That which we do not bring to consciousness appears in our lives as fate." He taught that repressed and rejected parts of ourselves appear in our dreams as antagonists and nightmare figures, which he called the shadow.

As dreamers, we greet all comers who knock at the door of our subconscious mind with curiosity. As writers, we can use whatever we encounter within us to create meaningful work on the page. And, if when we look into the shadows we find that there's just a friendly frog squatting on the windowsill, we can say hello, share a laugh, and awaken from our dread of the unknown with a smile—and a story to tell.

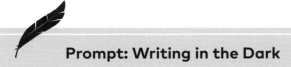

Writing isn't hard work, it's a nightmare.

—Philip Roth, novelist

Encounters with the shadow can be soul-shaking.

But the writer's compensation is that we can produce a literary gem from a dream that woke us up with a racing heart and clammy skin. Scary dreams also offer opportunities to explore the cobwebbed corners of our personalities and ultimately step into the warm glow of insight and understanding.

Try this: Rewrite a scary dream from the third-person point of view (*she, he, they* instead of *I*). Notice how shifting to the third person allows you to stay with the story longer, so you can discover its literary potential—and perhaps a healing perspective as well.

WRITING INTO (AND OUT OF) EMOTION

Is being burnt a requisite for the making of art?
Personally, I don't think it is. But art is poultice
for a burn. It is a privilege to have, somewhere
within you, a capacity for making something
speak from your own seared experience.

—Molly Peacock, *The Paper Garden:*
Mrs. Delany Begins Her Life's Work at 72

From the Inside Out

Soon after participants in a Dreaming on the Page workshop shrug off their jackets, drop their bags and backpacks to the ground beside them, or after they log into class on the computer, adjust their screens and volume levels, I start by asking each one to say how they feel. Whether we are meeting in person or online, those moments when we take turns putting our feelings into words may be the first time that day—or in several days—that they've had a moment to reflect on their emotional landscape.

Often they say they feel hungry, tired, or stressed. I listen to their answers and then encourage them to dig a little deeper to uncover the core emotion behind the generalized feeling of unease. "What does being exhausted or stressed make you feel?" I might ask. Perhaps someone is frustrated because they had to get to work early or stay late, and so they didn't get a chance to sit down and eat a proper meal all day. Another breath. Another moment. And now they can name what they are feeling as anger. Frustration has a fuzzy amorphous buzz to it. Anger carries with it information—a boundary was violated, or a need went unmet. With practice, we learn to feel the feeling, identify its source, reclaim a boundary perhaps, state our needs clearly, and, for the moment at least, move on.

The four basic emotions—*anger, sadness, gladness,* and *fear*—like primary colors, are the basis for all the others. Stress can be a mix of anger and fear, for example. Anxiety may contain fear and anger but also a little gladness mixed in. There is no right or wrong here. The answers will be different for each person, and they may vary from day to day. For now, we sit with the emotions until we feel which one is predominant. It might take a try or two before participants can identify what they're feeling, but when they do, they're rewarded. We can respond more effectively to what is happening outside of us—in our relationships at home, with friends, and at work, for example—when we know which feelings are stirring inside us.

Touching in with emotions is the first step toward making what's unconscious conscious—which, after all, is the goal of both dreamwork and writing.

But while emotional fluency is an essential skill for writers, I never heard it spoken of during my MFA studies, and it is rarely, if ever, addressed directly in most writing workshops. And yet, a story that lacks an emotional center falls flat and leaves both reader and writer empty.

Working with dreams, which run on emotions, can help us become more fluent in their language of self-expression. In REM sleep, when most memorable dreams take place, our amygdala (the part of the brain where strong feelings originate) is highly activated. So, dreams offer a nightly peek into the feelings that are arising within us. They color the mood of the dream and propel the plotline forward. A wave of happiness can paint our dreams in crystalline blues, and a rush of fear can turn the dreamscape into a dungeon-gray pit of terror. Those same emotions color the stories we tell ourselves and those we tell others about ourselves and the world as we perceive it.

We experience the effects of subterranean emotions on our thoughts and actions when we "wake up on the wrong side of the bed" and can't seem to get on the right footing all day long. When we acknowledge that it may have been a disturbing dream, remembered or not, that is dragging us down, we can begin to move through our feelings, rather than just drown them in a few cups of coffee.

As Tenzin Wangyal Rinpoche, a master of Tibetan dream yoga, a spiritual approach to developing lucid awareness during sleep and dreams, has written, "With experience of the dreamy and malleable nature of experience, we can transform depression into happiness, fear into courage, anger into love, hopelessness into faith, distraction into presence. What is dark we can change to light."

There is no grief in the house
of one who serves the muse.

—Sappho, poet of ancient Greece

How Are You?: Making an Everyday Question into a Daily Practice

How are you today? It seems like such a simple question on the surface. But it isn't always easy to answer. But if we take a breath and check inside for an honest answer, the question becomes an opportunity to wake up into the present moment rather than shoot back with an automatic (and meaningless) reply: "Fine." Be patient. Becoming proficient in the language of emotions takes time. Here are a few ways you can practice:

- This week, carry a notebook with you. Several times a day, jot down what you are feeling. Pause and try to distinguish which of the four basic emotions (anger, gladness, sadness, or fear) is at the root of generalized feelings such as anxiety, frustration, or confusion. To help you remember these root emotions, think: *Am I feeling mad, glad, sad, or afraid?*
- Review the writing in your journal and in your prose and poetry. Try to identify the emotions that are strongest.
- When writing your dreams, continue to identify the strongest emotion that's present in each one, as well as how you feel when you wake up.

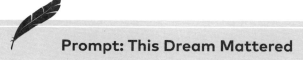

Write about a dream that helped you heal, a dream that woke you up to a new insight, or a time that writing helped you gain a new perspective or enriched your life from the inside out. Compose your story in a moving way that will help the reader understand the value of dreamwork or writing in your life. You might use these sentence starters to help you frame your story:

> *In this dream I* . . . [describe the dream]
> *Before this dream I* . . . [reflect on who you were, and how you behaved or thought differently before you had this dream]
> *Now I know* . . . [show through an example how you have grown or changed as a result of having paid attention to this dream]

WRITING
WITH ART

Collage is the twentieth
century's greatest innovation.

—Robert Motherwell, artist

With Scissors and Glue

When she was stuck on how to move the plot forward in her book *The Secret Life of Bees*, author Sue Monk Kidd sat down with scissors and glue and made a collage.

That night, she awoke near dawn and went to her study, where she contemplated the collage. "My eyes wander back and forth. . . . And boom, it falls out of the night, landing in one unbroken piece in my head," she wrote of her moment of inspiration.

"I was supposed to be writing an outline for the novel, and I was cutting out pictures," she wrote in *Traveling with Pomegranates*, a memoir she coauthored with her daughter, Ann Kidd Taylor. "I was thinking, this is nuts."

This description of an idea falling from the (midnight) blue, poetically describes how aha moments of clarity and insight so often drop into our minds in the hours between closing our eyes for bed and opening them again in the morning. Whether our answers are sent from the heavens or whether they bubble up from the neurochemical brew of our dreaming minds, the trick is to catch these insights and hold on. In this case, Kidd used a collage as a visual outline to help her complete the story she'd been wrestling with—and that story became an award-winning, bestselling book.

The poet John Ashbery, who also made collages, commented succinctly on the intersection between dreams and art in a published conversation with the poet John Yau. "In a number of your recent collages it's like you are about to undertake a journey or begin a dream," Yau said.

Ashbery replied: "That's how I feel much of the time."

The creative chaos of collage-making has much in common with the making of poetry and fiction—not to mention dreams. In each case, we make use of whatever is at hand: a swatch of buttery yellow, a long-ago memory, a bit of melancholy, a lick of rage, a curl of ribbon. Then, with the barest hint of a plan and the help of a glue-spattered muse, we arrange and rearrange the pieces until something vivid, new, and meaningful emerges.

Each snipped image and scrap of color contains its own context and web of associations. When assembled with other pieces, new sparks of narrative flare up, and the ever-shifting composition breaks free of its components to address some truth that extends beyond the sum of its parts.

Creating a collage from a dream has a similar effect. I like to contemplate a dream as I page through magazines for images and words that represent the characters, setting, and action it contained. This helps me slip past habitual patterns of thought as I place images on the page and rearrange them until I feel a hum of satisfaction that lets me know it's time to paste them down.

Collage is a form of improvisation. The exact right image can't be found or the bits of paper slip and stick in accidental configurations, and unexpected compositions jostle moods and meanings. The collage, once completed, is its own co-created dream. And that in turn can become the basis for a new poem or story, both indebted to and also unfettered from the dream that inspired it.

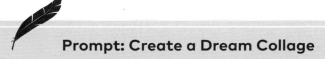

Prompt: Create a Dream Collage

When making a vision board, the aim is to select and collage images to manifest something new: perhaps a more loving relationship, a better job, or a bigger house. In dream collage, we do something different. We let go of any attempt to reproduce the dream faithfully. We mull over the emotional and visceral experience of it and allow impulse and intuition to guide the way. In this way we honor the fact that the dream may come true . . . but rarely in the ways we expect. Here's how to make a dream collage:

1. Set a timer for thirty to forty minutes. Keeping the process under an hour helps you squeeze past the internal censor so you can create freely.
2. While contemplating a dream, or a series of dreams on a particular theme, flip through magazines* and clip images you are drawn to. You don't need to know why you are choosing them or what they mean. Allow the subconscious mind to take over.
3. Arrange and rearrange the images until you feel satisfied, then paste them in place.
4. Rather than interpret or analyze the collage, admire and appreciate it. Trust that by touching in with the dream, and honoring it through your artistic creation, its healing message is being integrated into your life.

5. Use the collage as a prompt to create a poem or story. Gaze at it as if you are gazing into a new world and describe what you see.
6. Now, make a poem or story from your dream collage. Start with the words *In this dream I see* . . . and keep writing.

* If you don't have magazines to work with, you can download and print images from the internet or use old photographs, catalogues, or scraps of colored paper instead. Or contact a local school or library to see if they have magazines they'd be willing to pass on to you.

Prompt: Poetic Representation

I took my bed into the forest.
How peaceful, I thought,
When the moon came out.

—Charles Simic, "Henri Rousseau's Bed"

Ekphrastic poetry is written in response to a piece of visual art. The most famous example is "Ode on a Grecian Urn" by John Keats. You can use this form with dreams, too. For example, you can view a drawing, painting, or sculpture depicting a dream—made by you or another artist—and use it as inspiration to write a poem, as you did in the previous exercise with your dream collage.

Find an image online of a piece of artwork inspired by a dream. For example, look at Rousseau's classic *The Dream*, in which a woman sleeps on a sofa outdoors amid a landscape alive with foliage and wildlife. Charles Simic's poem (quoted above) and Sylvia Plath's poem "Yadwigha, on a Red Couch, Among Lilies" offer examples of ekphrastic responses to Rousseau's painting.

Try this:

1. Choose a dream-inspired artwork to respond to—or use Rousseau's widely accessible painting *The Dream.*
2. Spend time studying it. Pay special attention to the colors, characters, and activity it contains.
3. Write a descriptive poem or paragraph starting with the phrase *In this dream I see . . .* You can repeat that phrase as often as you like as you move through your poem.

GIVING FORM
TO WRITING

> *The motions he went through were few and always the same; they were really quite ordinary motions, which he had continually to practice in the day-time in the half-dark tent in order to retain his shackled freedom. In that he remained entirely within the limits set by his rope he was free of it, it did not confine him, but gave him wings. . . .*
>
> —Ilse Aichinger, "The Bound Man"

Thirsty for Words: Giving Form to Your Content

With my ubiquitous bottle of spring water held high, I introduce the day's lesson about form and content to the teen mothers in my poetry class. "This bottle of water can tell us a lot about how to write well," I say.

"Good, because I'm thirsty," Jessica says. Her sleepy smile is well earned. She has a three-month-old daughter in the daycare center downstairs and a toddler at home in her grandmother's care. Her curled eyelashes lift slowly toward the ceiling, as if they are tasked with lifting a heavy weight. The effect is charming, though I imagine that in this case it is meant as a minor mutiny. But I try to stay focused on my lesson plan.

"Okay, Jessica, you're thirsty. You want water. But what if I had plenty of water, but not the bottle? What then?"

"Just so long as you don't spill that on my desk, I am not trying to get my papers wet so I have to do all this homework again," says Siera, who is seated beside Jessica. I now see she is doing math problems that are due next period.

At least they are listening. It's not always easy to get my students' attention.

"So, the bottle is as important as what's inside of it, right?"

"As long as I get a drink when you're done talking about that water," says Jessica.

"Which raises a good point, thank you," I say. "Because this bottle is ideal for quenching one person's thirst. But, if I want to share, I need a different container, right?" I invite Jessica to go into the hall and bring back some paper cups from the watercooler. Then, I crack open the plastic cap and pour water from my bottle into each one. I hand out the cups of water and explain that form and content are equally important to writing. Just as we need the proper form to contain and share the water, so we need to find the right form to hold the content of our thoughts and ideas: Do we need an essay? A novel? A poem? Will the quaint confines of a couplet do? Or does our message require stanzas of more substantial length?

Sometimes content dictates the form. A haiku is perfect for containing a moment glimpsed in nature, just as a blue ceramic cup that fits snugly in the palm of the hand is ideal for a small serving of green tea. A life's story may need an epic form to hold it.

Once my students' thirst for water is sated, we pick up our pens and begin.

Transforming base metals into gold was the goal of alchemy, a branch of medieval chemistry. Creativity can be seen as an alchemical process, too, in which we transform the mundane into the magnificent and the everyday into the extraordinary. Any fiery and cataclysmic process, whether the alchemy of long-ago chemists or contemporary writers, requires a sturdy vessel to contain the explosive act of creation.

Up until now, we've focused on producing content. Now we'll look to the literary vessels that can contain creative experiments. We'll consider the range of forms available to hold our content and we'll recognize that dreams, which on the surface seem to ramble without a plan, actually have their own intrinsic structure.

In the prompts that follow, we'll honor the sturdy walls and safety that form provides so that our unpredictable words can—paradoxically—be free.

Prompt: Plot Holder

Usually, we remember only part of a dream, so we don't always see the scaffolding that supports our nightly narratives. Jung mapped out four parts of the dream like this:

Exposition. The situation, including setting, characters, and themes, are presented. *I dream I'm in a train station in a foreign country headed to an important meeting with my teachers.*

Development. The plot is set in motion as a problem arises and various solutions are tested. *I ask a porter to point me in the right direction for my train, but he shakes his head and says he's never heard of the town whose name is printed on my ticket. I run through the station asking various other officials how to find my train, all with the same result.*

Culmination. The course of action is completed and a climax is reached. *I venture outdoors and find a bus terminal. I approach a driver and fumble through my papers to hand her my ticket. The papers fall to the curb, and when I bend down to pick them up, I see that the driver's shoes are sparkling with dancing points of light.*

Lysis. In Jungian terms, lysis refers to the point when the result of the action on the dream protagonist is revealed, and even reinforced, by an infusion of a strong emotion. *I realize this is no ordinary bus terminal, and I have located someone who can transport me—perhaps with supernatural powers—to my destination. I feel overjoyed and I have a sense that this will be no ordinary journey.*

Now apply Jung's narrative structure to your dreams:

1. Study a series of your dreams. Can you detect any of these four narrative elements within their structure: exposition, development, culmination, lysis?

2. How does your view of your dreams change when you realize that while you sleep your brain gives them narrative structure? Reflect on this question in your journal.
3. Then, using a bit of reverse engineering, write a short story based on a dream, using the structure outlined above as the scaffolding for your story. You'll probably need to fill in missing or forgotten scenes. Go ahead! Use your imagination freely and have fun!

Give Your Dream a Title

At the start of Dreaming on the Page workshops, each member shares a dream title. Face it, dreams can be epic, overwhelming, confusing, and confounding. Giving them titles is a great way to touch in with a dream and sometimes even distill its essence in an instant. When we announce these short phrases in our circle—even before voicing the dreams in their entirety—we welcome their creativity, variety, humor, and aliveness into our midst.

Here are more reasons we title dreams as part of the Dreaming on the Page approach:

- The daily act of giving dreams titles is good practice for giving titles to our creative works.
- Titles help us distill the theme or home in on the central image, character, or action of a dream.
- In dreams and writing, effective titles hint at the contents of the text that follows.
- Titles point to more than one available meaning and hint at a variety of interpretations and poetic possibilities.
- A dream title at the top of the page helps you locate dreams in your journal as you flip through the pages, and reviewing a series of titles might also help you identify themes or patterns that emerge over time.
- When you return to a dream after doing some dreamwork with it, or after some time has passed, you can revise the title if it seems outdated. This simple act of revision highlights the fact that new insights on or perspectives about dreams are always possible.
- Dream titles add a creative and sometimes playful element to your dream journal.

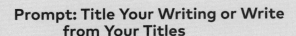

Dream titles can also serve as ready-made prompts. But if you don't have enough dream titles to work with, open a book of poetry or short stories to the table of contents and use those titles for the exercises that follow. Or use the titles of songs on a CD, album, or playlist:

Title poem. Look through your journal, and write the dream titles on strips of paper. Rearrange the titles into a poem. Edit lightly as needed.

Title prompt. Use a dream title as a writing prompt. Start a poem or paragraph with it.

THE
POETIC DREAM

Don't Call It Poetry

Emily Dickinson was a poet; no argument there. But in her lifetime, she published only about a dozen poems.

I have published dozens more than that, but I can safely say that no one will remember me for my verse. Still, I consider myself a poet no matter how many poems I write. Being a poet is less about the stanzas I inscribe on the page and more about a sensibility that reading and writing helps me cultivate. Poetry and dreams speak with the voice of the soul. For me, then, living soulfully is part of living poetically.

Poetry reminds us that there's more to life than business and bottom lines. I bring the soulful call of poetry to whatever work I do. When I was a journalist for a county newspaper, I used my time covering selectmen's meetings and the construction of new sewage plants as an opportunity to hone my skills of observation, and I trained my ear to listen closely for the most telling and memorable quote when interviewing local politicians or celebrities who were passing through our small city. In my years writing for newspapers, I even viewed the mandatory inverted-pyramid style as training for my forays into writing in poetic form. The necessity of writing within strict word counts pushed me to rely on the power of a single image to carry the emotional impact of an apartment fire or what was at stake in a contentious school board meeting—rather than falling into the wordiness of explication.

Greening my prose (cutting unnecessary words throughout a document, rather than lopping off large blocks of text) to fit the constraints of column inches and writing headlines to conform to character counts trained me in concision. Meanwhile, the necessity of churning out coherent copy on deadline prepared me to regard writer's block as a luxury I couldn't afford.

Then, after ten years in journalism, I went to graduate school for my formal training in writing. Although I wanted to get my degree in poetry, my partner, who would be paying our mortgage while I was in school, argued persuasively in favor of being more practical. An MFA in creative nonfiction became our compromise. But when I got to campus, I enrolled in so many poetry workshops (while still managing to eke out enough credits in my concentration) that the poetry students mistook me for one of them.

Fast-forward another decade or so, when I pursued yet another two-year course of study: this time a certification in dreamwork. Here I learned how to read and interpret the nightly narratives of our midnight minds. And there it was again: the power of imagery, the transformational magic of metaphor, and the way the proximity of seemingly unrelated objects, characters, or actions in dreams sparked unexpected insights. I couldn't help but marvel at the similarities between dream reports and poems.

These days when I teach, the word *dream* sometimes escapes from my lips when I mean to say *poem*, or *poem* pops out when I mean to say *dream*. I consider these so-called Freudian slips as examples of getting the wrong word right. My mind wisely refuses to acknowledge the difference. Poetry is dreaming on the page. Dreaming is the spontaneous poetry of our sleeping mind.

That's why when students in my writing classes tell me that they aren't poets, I tell them, "Just write what is in your heart then, and don't call it poetry." And when students in my dream classes tell me that they don't remember any dreams, I suggest they look to a poem instead—read one or write one—and then, they are a dreamer, too.

In this section you'll wax poetic, whatever your genre. But first, let's clarify what I mean by poetry. For our purposes it is:

- Writing, whether in a stanza or a prose paragraph, that brings a bright beam of consciousness to language and contains vivid imagery and honest emotion.
- Writing that celebrates the sounds of speech, as well as the musicality and rhythm of the human voice and the human heart.
- Writing that awakens the senses, including sight, hearing, smell, taste, and touch/feeling—and an overall soulful sensibility.

Prompt: Dream Up a Poem

Here's a quick way to find the poetry in your dream reports:

1. Select a dream from your journal that contains strong imagery and emotion—two key poetic ingredients.
2. Rewrite the dream in the present tense, as if it is happening now, using descriptive language and active, original, or precise verbs.
3. Delete unnecessary words.
4. Insert line breaks.
5. Edit lightly if needed . . . and presto! You've written a poem.

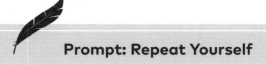

Prompt: Repeat Yourself

In writing, repetition can either be a red flag alerting us that revision is needed—or it can be a tool to wield skillfully. As with redundancy in writing, recurring dreams can mean we're retelling the same tired story with no new insights. But, if we pay attention, we'll find that recurring dreams can also wake us up to issues we need to address so we can revise our lives to lead us to happier endings.

By contrast, we can capitalize on repetition in our writing to create sustaining rhythms, purposefully returning to key lines and phrases to deepen their meaning. Likewise, through dreamwork we can turn recurring dreams into gold as we receive their messages, incorporate their wisdom, and take appropriate actions in response. To avoid dull and unproductive redundancies in writing and to resolve recurring dreams, approach each one with awareness.

The pantoum, villanelle, sestina, and triolet are examples of poetic forms that use repetition artistically. But you don't have to learn complicated patterns and rhyme schemes to get the benefits. Instead, you can make up your own poetic form:

1. Choose five lines from different dreams and repeat them, varying their order to create a ten- to twenty-line poem.
2. Loosen your grip on what the poem means and let the repeating lines lead where they may.
3. Notice how an incantatory pattern can call attention to sounds and images as they recur and inspire new meanings.
4. Edit your poem lightly so that it is satisfying and meaningful.

Prompt: A Playful Challenge

Writing in form can induce a productive dreamy state: The rules focus the logic- and order-loving prefrontal cortex on counting syllables and tallying up lines, while the creative right brain can run freely beneath the radar of our internal censor. As a result, the dream reveals itself in new and surprising ways.

You don't have to be fluent in iambs and dactyls or even know what a poetic foot is in order to enjoy experimenting with form.

Try rewriting a dream report using a traditional poetic form, such as the villanelle, sonnet, or ode.

For helpful descriptions of various poetic forms, consult these resources:

- *The Teachers and Writers Handbook of Poetic Forms* is an accessible reference guide.
- Poets.org provides an excellent online resource on poetic form, too. (Note the entries for pantoum, sestina, sonnet, and aisling.) https://poets.org/glossary/

There's another alphabet, whispering
from every leaf, singing from every river,
shimmering from every sky.

—Dejan Stojanovic, Serbian poet

Informed by the Alphabet

I am always searching for meaning. Everyday events, like a yellow-gold leaf drifting down from an autumn tree and landing on my shoulder during my morning walk, might carry some message. Dreams and poetry teach us the language of symbol and metaphor. As we become more literate in these alternate alphabets, we are better able to give expression to what was otherwise beyond the power of ordinary words to say.

The symbolic alphabet of dreams, like that of poetry, helps us read more deeply into the world of everyday experience. The next prompt invites you to reconsider your ABCs to find new meaning in the offbeat logic of dreams.

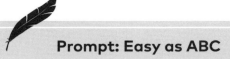

Prompt: Easy as ABC

The abecedarian is a poetic form in which each line or stanza begins with a letter of the alphabet, starting with *A* and progressing to *Z*. Write a dream poem using the abecedarian form. You might write about a single dream or a series of dreams in this way, or you might choose to contemplate your experience of the night, as you flow through the alphabet. You can start each line with:

A is for . . .
B is for . . .
C is for . . .

. . . and so on, filling in each line with images from your dreams that start with that letter, or using that letter of the alphabet to describe your dreams in a more general way.

Learn about the pine from the pine.
Learn about the bamboo from the bamboo.

—Basho, Japanese poet

Haiku: The Ancient Art of Tweetable Poems

Flash fiction, flash memoir, and tiny love stories seem to be trending these days. But haiku has helped poets travel light for centuries. At three lines and seventeen syllables, nothing is wasted. There is room for an awareness and a bit of action and nothing more. You observe the bamboo; you don't explain it.

Dreams, too, are an ancient form of storytelling. And despite their reputation for rambling, they are also expert in the art of condensation. As anyone who has done dreamwork knows, a one-page dream report can result in five pages of association and explication—proving that there is a big story hidden inside of even a brief dream.

Dream haiku combines the best of both creative forms. But if your seventh-grade English class ruined haiku for you, call these tweetable poems, or flash verse, instead. And speaking of seventh grade, don't worry about the syllable counts or line limits you may have learned back then. We're not keeping count. Instead, we'll focus on these key features of haiku:

- Haiku is rooted in nature and, and like dreams, often reveals something about human nature.
- Haiku, like dreams, are tiny nuggets of wide-eyed attention, wrapped in imagery and emotion.
- Haiku, in its brevity, offers the perfect balance to dreams' often-lengthy narratives.
- Haiku always contains a twist or a surprise—as does a good dream.

Practice writing these tiny poems to train yourself to use imagery, emotion, compression, creativity, and the art of surprise in your writing, whatever your genre.

Prompt: Write a Dream Haiku

Haiku is commonly defined by syllable counts, but haiku is not about math. Focus instead on distilling meaning into images and very few words. Here's how:

1. Write down the dream you want to work with.
2. Bypass explanation and editorializing and focus instead on a bold image and an action.
3. Surprise yourself (and your reader) in the last line. This can come in the form of a subtle twist or a bright splash of astonishment.
4. Eliminate some more! Can you pare down your poem to about three lines? Something that would fit into a tweet?
5. Create dream haiku on a regular basis as an exercise in gleaning insight from your dreams, as well as to practice the art of poetry.

DREAMING OFF THE PAGE

Be Not Contained Between Your Hat and Boots

This kind of thing happens all the time: Someone tells me they write—maybe even every day—but then hurry to make sure I don't think they're a *writer*. They tell me they love poetry—reading it and writing it—but alas, I should not by any means presume they are a *poet*. Over and over people tell me they don't remember their dreams, or that they don't dream at all—even though science tells us that everybody dreams several times each night.

But when we speak of our urge to write or our desire to dream, it's not about claiming a field of expertise or even excellence. It is about seeing the world anew each day. It's about honoring our heart's desires. It's about dreaming up new possibilities for our individual lives and our world.

There are risks to denying the dreamy and creative parts of ourselves, too. To be a poet, a writer, and a dreamer is our birthright, and to deny these parts of ourselves is to deny our full humanity.

We can look to the poets to teach us how to reclaim these essential parts of ourselves. Walt Whitman, in the preface to *Leaves of Grass*, offers these instructions on how to be a poet. As you read these lines, notice that there's no mention of MFAs, or writing workshops, or even pen and paper. To be a poet, Whitman says:

> Love the earth and sun and the animals, despise riches, give alms to everyone that asks, . . . devote your income and labor to others, hate tyrants, argue not concerning God, have patience and indulgence toward the people . . . re-examine all you have been told in school or church or in any book, and dismiss whatever insults your own soul; and your very flesh shall be a great poem.

These could as easily be instructions for how to be a dreamer, or any kind of creative soul.

Prompt: How to Be a Dreamy Poet

Reflecting on the instructions offered by these writers, consider your relationship to dreams and writing. Can you honor yourself as a dreamer, even when you haven't remembered a dream in months? Are you a writer only when you have your fingers on the keyboard or a pen in your hand? Can you live like a writer and a dreamer even when you are out in an open field or walking up a city block alone? How?

1. Craft a statement about what it means to live a poetic and dreamy life, whether or not you remember your dreams, and whether you write in stanzas or in paragraphs. What are the values, sensibilities, and daily actions you take to live a soulful life?
2. Let these lines spark your own:

    To be a [poet/writer/dreamer/creative soul], *I need . . .*
    I must make a place for . . .
    I depend upon . . .
    I shun . . .
    I must communicate . . .
    I don't know . . .
    I do know . . .

Part Three

FROM PILLOW TO PUBLISHED

In addition to shaping my pedagogy as a writing instructor, my dreams have also helped me navigate my career. I've had dreams that led me to jobs, boosted my confidence on the job, and told me when it was time to quit a job. For example, after long consideration, I knew when it was time to leave my position teaching poetry to teen mothers and launch my dreamwork business after I had a dream that took place in an airport, where I saw a sign that said that my flight had been cleared for takeoff. I also received the name for my new business in a dream when a stranger I met on a street corner in my dreamscape handed me a flyer for an upcoming event. I looked down and read the words *Third House Moon* printed across the top of the page.

"What's this?" I asked.

"It's your new business, and it's going to be successful," she said.

Dreams + Action = Change

—Justina Lasley, *Wake Up to Your Dreams*

Third House Moon? What did that even mean? When I woke up I googled the phrase and learned that when the moon appears in the third house of someone's astrological chart it means that they are likely to be imaginative and intuitive. I asked a friend who understands astrology to identify where the moon is on my natal chart. It's not in the third house, as it turns out. But that didn't mean my dream had led me astray. The description of the qualities associated with a third-house moon was consistent with my vision for my budding new business as an enterprise that would honor and encourage the development of intuition, and it underlined my desire to communicate and work with others. According to one website I consulted: "Others may view you as a bit of a dreamer. You have a knack for putting the feelings of a group into words, and may serve as a teacher or spokesperson." Bingo!

And so the name stuck. I had it printed on my business cards and return address stamp, and I filed business papers for my LLC using it. After all, it isn't *just* a dream if we act on it.

It's easy to see that dreams assist us with right-brained creative pursuits such as writing. But this dream reminds me that when it comes to the business of, well, business, we shouldn't leave our dreams behind. It's instructive to remember that dreams serve people with pocket protectors and microscopes as much as those who pen poems. Danish physicist Niels Bohr had a dream that led him to discover the structure of the atom. Madam C. J. Walker (Sarah Breedlove) claimed that the formula for a hair tonic for Black women came to her in a dream. That concoction, by the way, was the start of the beauty empire she built and which, in the late 1800s, made her the first Black millionaire. More recently, the idea for Google came to Larry Page, another highly successful inventor, in a dream. As for literature, we've already established that the list of dream-inspired works of fiction and poetry could, well, fill a book. But dreams have also helped authors with the business end of writing: from preparing manuscripts to bringing them to market.

My mentor in dream leadership, Justina Lasley, founder of the Institute for Dream Studies, teaches that *Dreams + Action = Change*. She understands that, despite the stereotype of dreamers as idealists who lack practical skills and training, the truth is that there are effective ways to bring the benefits of dreams and dreamwork into all aspects of our lives. Dreams *do* come true when we take them off the pillow and take action on the messages they bring us. As writers, we manifest dreams when we dress them up in words and arrange them on the page. We continue to dream them into being when we edit, revise, and make our work public.

Airlift

I was several weeks into a Dreaming on the Page workshop, when a participant raised her hand: "I've filled a notebook. Now what?" Good question. By this point in the DOTP process you, too, have likely produced reams of dreamy writing, and you might be wondering the same thing. The first step is to lift selected bits of writing out of your journals and notebooks. Here's how I've adapted the process that Judy Reeves, author of *A Writer's Book of Days*, calls "airlifting":

1. Block out time on your calendar monthly or quarterly to review your journals.
2. Settle on the floor or at a table large enough to spread out your notebooks.
3. Use colored pens, sticky notes, and index cards to flag or copy out poetic lines, insights, characters, plotlines, or imagery from dreams and other journal entries.
4. Create electronic or paper files to sort and organize your material by project, theme, or topic—or whatever system suits your needs.
5. Refer to your files as you write, and incorporate your air-lifted pieces into ongoing projects, or start something new based on what you've retrieved from your notebooks.

> *You know what the difference is*
> *between a dream and a goal? A plan.*

— Jodi Picoult, novelist

Bringing Your Dreams to Market

I was ankle-deep in manuscript pages with a deadline looming and pressure mounting, when I asked myself, "Whose bright idea was it to write a book anyway?"

Dreaming up the idea for the book was fun, as was researching my topic, and brainstorming chapter headings and a title. But now I had that long-awaited contract in hand, and suddenly every time I sat down to write I had a heavy feeling in my chest and doubts clouded my thoughts. Rushing to make a deadline and trying to mold my ideas to fit the metrics of my publisher's marketing department were draining my energy. Ironically, the book I was writing was titled *Joy in Every Moment*, and it was about how to cultivate everyday happiness. Except that I was no longer experiencing much joy in producing it. I realized that tapping into my dreamy imagination came naturally when I was putting pen to paper and generating new ideas. But now, as I was getting down to the business of polishing my words and preparing my work for publication, I had consigned my right-brain intuition-fueled creativity to a dusty corner of my mind. And then, *pfffft*. That's the sound of joy leaking out of my heart.

I had to remind myself of my own philosophy: Happiness is an inside job, and sometimes it takes work to reclaim our joyful lives. If writing a book about joy was going to be joyful, I would have to follow my own advice.

So, before I edited another page, I stopped focusing on the finished product and paused to consider how I wanted to experience this phase of the publishing process. I knew right away that I wanted to bring a spirit of playfulness to the task. I got out my colored pens and pastel-hued sticky notes, because making revisions in pink and purple and marking pages with shades of springtime makes me happy.

I also wanted to bring my love of ritual to the process, so I shopped for a talisman that I could put on my desk to remind me of my intentions. In the children's section of a bookstore, I found a set of wooden alphabet letters mounted on stainless steel wheels to look like train cars. Button-sized magnets let me connect a purple *J*, a blue *O*, and a yellow *Y*, to make a bright *JOY* train. When I got home, I gave *J.O.Y.* a place of honor on my writing desk, literally. Each time I looked at it, a wave of gladness rose up in me, reminding me that the business of creativity didn't have to be dreary.

Dreamwork, too, affirms that process is as important as the finished product. So, when it comes to revising and selling a book, we can infuse our work with soulful purpose and joy, too.

Ready. Set. Action.

To continue living a dream-centered life, even when it's time to get down to business, bring dream incubation and a splash of color to your next project. Here's how:

1. **Incubate it**. Ask your dreams for guidance on your next project, whether it's writing an essay, poem, story, book, or blog—and whether you're just beginning, or if you're ready to bring your work out into the world, sign a contract, or create marketing materials.*
2. **Cut and paste**. Create a collage based on images from the dream you incubated in step 1. You can use your collage as a visual synopsis or outline of your book, story, essay, or poem. Or look to it to gain new perspective or guidance on any aspect of the business of writing.

3. **Shop for it**. Purchase a totem or touchstone based on the dream you incubated. Let that object be a tangible reminder of what you want to manifest.

4. **A special place**. Arrange objects that remind you of your intentions on a project altar. This can be a corner of your desk, a windowsill, or mantel where you place any or all of the following: a totem or touchstone, your dream collage, power stones or crystals, a candle or fairy lights. What else might you add?

5. **Book it**. Make a project notebook where you track any related ideas, inspirations, and dream wisdom. Keep your markers, glue stick, and magazines handy, because this notebook should be full of color and creativity and it should bring you joy each time you open it!

* For more on how to incubate dreams, see Dream Incubation Basics in the appendix (page 236).

We talked of mice, the cat and I,

and of the importance of napping.

—Catherine Gilbert Murdock, *The Book of Boy*[9]

Power Naps with a Purpose

Jacqueline Sheehan came to me for a session because she wasn't remembering her dreams. It wasn't the first time someone came to me for guidance on dream recall, but this was different. Sheehan, a bestselling author whose many novels include *Lost and Found* and *Now and Then*, depends on her dreams. It's not unusual, of course, for an author to look to her dreams for inspiration, but for Sheehan dreams are essential to the process. "If I'm not connected to my dreams, I really can't write," she said.

Happily, after just one session of our work together, her dream drought ended, and her writing blossomed again (which happens frequently for my dreamwork clients).

Sheehan first understood the power of her dreams when she was still working as a psychologist and living in California. She didn't even consider herself a writer when she dreamed of a dark-skinned woman sitting beneath a white birch tree with three trunks. The image "came out of nowhere." Whoever this was, Sheehan knew this character had a story to tell.

She didn't yet know that the dream was giving her a glimpse of the heroine of her first novel, *Truth*, based on the life of Sojourner Truth, who escaped slavery and became an activist for abolition and women's rights. Nor did she know then that when she moved across the country in 1995 to settle in Florence, Massachusetts, she'd be living just blocks from the house where, in the mid-nineteenth century, Truth had lived for fourteen years. As for the birch tree with its tripled trunk, to Sheehan it came to mean that her job was to present the many aspects of this woman's personality. The publication of Sheehan's historical novel in 2003 did just that. She told Truth's multifaceted story, and her dreams have guided her writing ever since.

But Sheehan doesn't just wait for dreams to come—she invites them. She uses dream incubation to prompt ideas for books, titles, and insights into her characters' inner lives. On a typical writing day, Sheehan might pause for a twenty- to thirty-minute nap on the cozy gold-and-maroon-colored sofa in her living room. Before she closes her eyes, she poses a question about a character or a plot she's grappling with. She drops quickly into sleep and wakes with renewed clarity. Sometimes she receives a dream image that informs what she'll write that afternoon.

In one instance, she was writing about a character, Lily, who, at twenty-nine, learned she was adopted. "I needed to capture more of her emotions toward her adopted mother, who she had always thought was her biological mother," Sheehan said. Then, during a nap, she was able to see through the eyes of her character. "It let me be Lily for a little time, and feel what Lily must have been feeling."

Another time, she was agonizing over what to title the book she was working on. During a nap, the words *now and then* came to mind, and she knew that would be the title of her book about time travel.

If the naps create small spaces of insight, her nighttime dreams spin out entire narratives. Sometimes they even spin out of control. Once, dream characters were clamoring so insistently for a role in the book she was writing that she had to tell many of them that, no, she couldn't include them. Although not everything that comes to her in a dream makes it onto the page, Sheehan says she can't imagine writing without that access to the inspiration they provide.

"I wish I could let every writer know that they have this and they can use this," she said. "If you have a question about something in your writing, if it feels as if something has yet to be revealed or illuminated, write it down before bed," Sheehan advises. "I give myself the suggestion that I will allow myself to dream about it, and that I'll remember the dream and write it down."

Incubation Anytime

You don't have to take a nap or wait until bedtime to get dreamy support from your subconscious mind. Try this:

1. Any time of day, pose a question about the problem or issue you're having with your work.
2. Write the question down. Then put the pen down and go do the dishes, fold the laundry, or water the plants. In short, do anything that doesn't involve paper, pen, or print in any form.
3. Let your question settle into the back of your mind where your dreamy subconscious mind can work on it without your conscious involvement. Let go and see what manifests when you return to the desk.

> *And that's why you have to be lonely so that the unconscious becomes stronger.*
>
> —Marie-Louise Von Franz, from the film *Matter of the Heart*

Table for One

Mealtimes became a challenge during the years I lived alone, after my daughter went off to college, and my then-partner left to follow a different path. Dinners morphed from sit-down affairs to sandwiches or bowls of cereal eaten while standing over the sink.

Then I realized that feeding myself didn't have to be a chore. Instead, preparing new recipes with care and rediscovering what satisfied my taste buds became a ritual of self-care. Sitting at my dining room table set for one, with a cloth napkin and a candle on most nights, became an opportunity to enjoy my own company. I even began going out to restaurants alone, and when the hostess would ask, "Just one?" I'd stand up a little straighter and say, "Yes, a table for one," consciously, and confidently, dropping the *just*.

Similarly, writing "*just* for yourself" doesn't have to be the equivalent of standing over the sink at dinnertime scarfing down a PB&J sandwich. Writing is always an act of solitude, but that makes it more valuable, not less. So, we shouldn't treat pieces we compose *just* for ourselves like proverbial neglected stepchildren, lavishing all of our literary attention on the darlings we send out for publication. Any writing we do has the potential to nourish. The writing that is meant for our eyes only can be particularly valuable because we cultivate our capacity to notice what inspires us, and what's worth putting into words so we can preserve it, revisit it, and take the time to know it more deeply—without regard to whether others would understand or appreciate it.

Searching for just the right word, spending time massaging a sentence until it sings, and rediscovering what inspires you can be its own universe of joy and fulfillment separate from seeing your work in print. And for some of us, that is not only *enough*, it's a deliciously satisfying and complete creative experience.

Deciding to remain single is a strong and healthy stance when it comes from a place of positivity and self-acceptance and not from a pit of disappointment and bitterness. So, too, deciding that you are writing purely for yourself can be an empowered stance—if it comes from a place of self-love and not low self-esteem.

Before claiming certainty about whether to keep your dreamy writing in the drawer rather than prepare it for a wider audience, pause to get clear on this point: Are you writing only for yourself because you're not sure your work is good enough to share with others? Or is this a conscious decision, lovingly made to cultivate a productive and solitary pursuit?

Journal about your choice to write for an audience of one, and talk it over with a trusted friend. If it is a choice made from self-regard, celebrate it! But if it's a familiar yet unwelcome voice telling you you're not good enough that is dictating this choice, consider taking even a small step toward making your writing public.

Here are some thoughts to consider:

Humble pie—or humble lie? Dreams present themselves to an audience of one, sure. But poems and stories are usually meant to have a wider reach. Ask yourself: Are you being humble when you say you don't want to share your writing? Or are you holding yourself back out of fear?

Manuscript destiny. Each piece of writing, as with each person, has its own destiny. It's your job to prepare your written work to enter the world in a way that allows it to fulfill its purpose. Ask yourself, what does this story or poem need to reach its full potential? Is it meant for me alone? Or is there a wider audience that would benefit from this piece? If so, build up your confidence and do your part to make it happen.

A generous act. Someone may have told you that writing is selfish. But, in fact, sharing your work is a generous act. Your words can inform and entertain others, and your writing can offer readers the chance to see themselves with more depth and clarity, too.

Publish Yourself

As a ten-year-old, I made my first foray into publishing when I carefully copied my poems on loose-leaf paper and arranged them in a red plastic binder, on whose cover I proudly wrote the word *POAMS* in black marker.

In my twenties, with the advent of personal computers and spellcheck (which I clearly needed), I learned to use a rudimentary desktop publishing program to design my own poetry chapbooks. I printed them and had them copied and staple-bound at a neighborhood copy shop, then gave them away as holiday gifts to friends and family.

My literary role models included Walt Whitman, who self-published his poems, and Emily Dickinson, who sewed hers into booklets she stowed in her dresser drawers (and which weren't discovered and published until after her death). I also loved that Charles Dickens first serialized his novels, one chapter at a time, in magazines.

You may have grown up believing that the only kind of publishing that counts is when you're signed by an agent who sells your work to one of the big houses, and all you need to do is sit back and collect fat royalty checks. But the word *publication*, at its root, has a modest definition: to make a piece of writing public. From papyrus to the printing press to print-on-demand technology, aspiring writers through the ages have used the technology of their times to get their words out. Nineteenth-century writers had broadsheets and serialization; writers today have e-newsletters, blogs, and subscription services such as Patreon and Substack (platforms come and go, so research the most current options) to connect with an audience even when a publishing contract eludes them.

These days, when traditional publishers seem leery of taking a chance on new writers, it's more important than ever to take advantage of creative options to forge your unique path to publishing success. Keep an open mind and find the option (or options) that suit your temperament and that best serve your writing. There's a wide range:

Take one small step. Ease into bringing your poems into the public eye by typing up your favorites and posting them on your refrigerator door where your family or closest friends might see them. Or post an essay to your social media pages, or send a story via email to a small circle of appreciative friends.

Post a poem. One of my students copies her poems onto postcards and sends them to her close circle of friends. Cecilia says, "My friends like receiving them, and it feels nice to share a poem out into the world in this small way. Otherwise it feels like my writing is a big secret." Try it, and let your creativity fly free!

Widen your circle. Host a reading in your home or at a community center for a group of friends, family members, your book club, or support group.

Pick up the mic. Sign up to read at an open mic or coffeehouse in your community or online.

Community connection. Publish a poem or story in a local newspaper or in a neighborhood newsletter.

Address an admiring blog. Feature your work in a weekly or monthly blog post or podcast.

Self-publish a chapbook. Gather a small collection of poems or stories, or polish off a novella or short memoir. Edit and print your work, and share it with your friends and social media followers. Your local bookstore or library might even agree to carry it.

Submit it. Research online and print journals, periodicals, or anthologies that are seeking submissions, and send yours out for publication.

Book it. Do you have a full-length collection of stories, poems, or essays? A novel or memoir you have long dreamed of publishing? Maybe it's time to consider publishing a book of your own.

Keep dreaming. What other options can you think of to make your work public in traditional—or new and creative—ways?

Nothing's worth seeing
that's not seen with fresh eyes.

—Basho, Japanese poet

Revision: No Red Pencil Needed

As a college student, I handed in a paper that was hastily typed and covered with penciled-in rewrites. My professor returned it to me, unread. But rather than berate me for my sloppiness (which would have been deserved), she said, "Give your writing the respect it deserves. Revise this, retype it, and hand it in again." I'd been dressed down more than once during my school years for my spelling errors and sloppy handwriting, but this professor's words stayed with me. I took her reproach to heart so much, in fact, that when I submitted my manuscript to an agent many years later, he commented that he'd never received such clean copy from an author before. And he took me on as a client.

So, I get it when the word *revision* strikes fear in a writer's heart. We conjure images of red slash marks through our precious lines of poetry, or harsh syllables scrawled by harried editors in the margins of our prose. But I've come to know that revision is really an opportunity to dress your words up in the spiffy suit of literary attire they deserve. Even if you never publish what you write, your words are worthy of the time and commitment needed to polish them up. What's more, completing a piece of writing, no matter how small, or how grand, is worthy of approbation and celebration. Yes, that means writing more than one draft, revising, and editing. Why? Because what you have to say—to yourself or to others—is worth getting right.

The good news is that just as our right-brain dreamy imagination has been our ally in the generative phase of the creative process, our dreams and subconscious mind can help us here, too. The concept of revision even appears in Freud's theory of dream construction. Secondary revision, as defined by Freud, is when conscious thought enters the production of the dream. The ego, like an editor on the night shift, tries to make the dream make sense. This, Freud says, is why some parts of a dream may seem illogical, while others are quite coherent. Whether or not this theory still holds water, it is interesting to note that revision has a function in dream formation. In my work, I notice that a series of dreams over the course of a single night, or over the course of weeks or even years, revisits certain themes and revises the stories we tell ourselves over time. After all, revision is a natural part of storytelling. Our inner editor is hard at work revising the stories we tell ourselves about our waking lives, too. Writing and dreaming are two ways that we make sense of the world and our place in it, and revising through therapy, dreamwork, and writing means we have a chance to continuously correct and continue.

Revision may be natural, and even essential, to success for writers, but that doesn't mean there's not hard work involved. Not only is it time-consuming, but there is always the fear of losing what is successful during revision, deleting the daring word in a moment of insecurity and settling instead for the commonplace. But once embarked upon, and fully embraced, revision is not only pleasurable, it can be profound. Think of it: What if we applied the lessons of revision and the bestowing of careful attention to detail onto the grandest composition of all: our lives? What would it mean to rewrite a single experience or gesture until we make it sing like the loveliest of poems? What new meanings might we find by re-envisioning, fine-tuning, and finessing the stories of our lives?

As we read *Anna Karenina,*
we are under the same
illusion of authorlessness
we are under as we follow
the stories that come to us
at night and seem to derive
from some ancient hidden
reality rather than from
our own, so to speak, pens.

—Janet Malcolm, *Nobody's Looking at You*

Re-visioning

Poet Mary Oliver has said that she rewrote her poems upwards of forty to fifty times before she considered them complete. You don't need to revise your work as many times as Oliver did. But be warned, once you awaken to the pleasures of revision, you just might want to. Here are some tips on how to approach revision:

Get the red out. If red pen marks on the page still make you sweat, mark up your work in green or purple ink, or with any color that helps you lighten up your relationship to the revision process.

Not-so-critical distance. There's a reason writers often hide their drafts away in a drawer for weeks or months before revising. We need some distance to help us see our work anew. Another way to achieve critical distance and ditch hypercritical habits of thinking is to shift your perspective. Read what you've written as if it's something you found in a favorite book, written by an author you admire. Approach your own writing with that same eager anticipation and curiosity you would a piece by a favorite author. Look for things to appreciate, before looking for things to improve.

A second set of eyes. Dream groups are valuable because others in the circle can easily see truths in our dreams that we cannot. Our blind spots prevent us from grasping the dream's otherwise obvious messages. The same goes for writing. Our stories and poems have lived in our heads for so long it can be difficult to see their strengths and weaknesses by ourselves. So, after revising on your own, ask a writer friend or someone who appreciates good literature to read your latest draft, and incorporate any helpful feedback.

It's important in life to conclude things properly. Only then can you let it go.

—Yann Martel, *Life of Pi*

Ending It

Some of my clients cringe when I suggest they make up a new ending to a dream that has left them hanging. Dreams, they argue, are too pure or precious to mess with.

I don't know about you, but if I were hanging by my fingernails high above a rocky ravine, I'd welcome a rewrite that includes a stranger with a sturdy arm who could pull me back onto solid ground. And fast.

Revising dreams is not only permissible, it can have healing benefits. For example, a highly effective dreamwork technique called image rehearsal therapy offers nightmare sufferers the opportunity to change the ending of the dream to something more positive, satisfying, or constructive. With guidance from a trained therapist, they then rehearse the new dream in their imagination until they have an updated relationship to the dream, and thus to themselves.

Dreaming up new endings to novels has been popularized by choose-your-own-adventure stories, in which alternate endings leave various possibilities open for the reader. Yann Martel, author of *Life of Pi*, challenges the traditional notions of endings, too. Martel weaves an improbable tale of a boy (the son of a zookeeper) who is lost at sea on a boat with an orangutan, a tiger, and a hyena and renders it believable with his skillful storytelling. But ultimately the reader is left to wonder what really happened. Martel prods us with this question: When in doubt, why not choose the better story? He invites us to consider that those familiar last words, *The End*, that stand like locked doors at the back of a book, may be replaced by revolving doors, or doors to which we have the key, so we can open them and explore for ourselves instead.

When it comes to our own lives, we can look for the better story within our experiences, too. Dreamwork and writing offer opportunities to reach new levels of truth by providing missing perspectives and new interpretations, for example. They afford us the chance to try on new endings for each chapter in our life stories, even as they are being written. With dream reentry, we can complete a dream, even if we wake before it has concluded. And writing lets us try out more satisfying endings, too. Consider these possibilities:

Happily ever after. Think of examples of endings that leave you feeling satisfied in poetry and prose. Are they the final scenes that answer all the questions or the ones that leave you with new perspectives and lines of inquiry? (Dreams usually favor the latter approach.) Now look at a piece of your own writing. Where does it end? Have you wrapped things up so tightly that you choke the life out of your work? Have you left room for the reader to draw conclusions of their own?

Come to a new conclusion. Review your dream journals, and notice how your dreams end. With dreams that leave you hanging—or that come to disturbing conclusions—try on different endings that let you practice new and healthier behaviors, or that affirm your power to stand up for yourself with confidence and poise. In a dream that wakes you up just as flames are consuming the kitchen, could you have found a fire extinguisher or called for help? In a dream where a beggar is holding out a bowl requesting alms, but you walked by without making an offering, can you return to the scene and find out what you have to give that might be of use? Is there something you might have said to resolve a troubling conversation? A question you wish you had asked? Rehearse the new dream ending in your mind several times a day for the next week, and see if it helps you live a little more happily ever after.

An Open-Ended Ending

On the morning that I was to write the conclusion to this section, I woke from a dream where I was in a meeting with a literary agent. Everything about her, from the silk blouse that draped over her thin frame to her expensive-looking slacks and smart leather flats, said that her time was valuable. From her formal body language, I knew that whatever our business together had been, my time with her was now over. Still, I had a question to ask and I wasn't about to waste this opportunity.

"Just one more thing," I said. She assessed me with a cool, professional gaze. But there was kindness in her eyes, too, so I went on: "I'd like to know what I should prioritize next: Writing poetry? A memoir? What would you recommend, given your understanding of the market?" I was breathless from trying to get my question out before she would, I feared, check her watch and indicate that it was time for her to move on.

"Sure, we can discuss that," she said.

And then, as the old story goes, I woke up.

I wrote the dream in my journal, feeling frustrated that I didn't get the answer to my question. I showered and went to meet my friend Lori for breakfast. Over steaming mugs of coffee, I told her about the chapter I'd been working on as well as the dream. "It would have been convenient if the dream had given me a clear answer, so I could conclude this section with a confident endorsement of the role dreams play in guiding literary careers," I told her.

"But don't you teach people that every character in a dream represents a part of themselves?" she asked.

"Sure, but . . ."

"So that literary agent is an aspect of you, right?"

"Well, yes." I blew on my coffee before taking a sip.

"Then you should definitely put it in your book. Use it to remind your readers that, as you keep telling me, dreams guide us to look inside ourselves, where the answers have been waiting all along."

Sometimes it's hard to take my own advice. But Lori was right. So, I have shared this dream to remind you (and me) that dream wisdom is *our* wisdom. Those wise dream advisors are parts of ourselves, only they may be dressed up in spiffier clothes sometimes. Trust your inner voice, whether it arrives in a dream, or in conversation with a close friend over coffee. Then take your writing in the direction of your dreams.

> *Many of the world's most beautiful poems*
> *are made to address an ache that can only*
> *be assuaged by describing it precisely.*
>
> —Anna Akhmatova, poet

On Drowning and Driving

During a writing class for immigrants, I worked with a young woman who had come to New England after fleeing violence in Central America. Sonia spoke so quietly that her classmates had to lean in to hear her, and she wrote in a tiny cursive script, as if she didn't want her words to take up any space on the page. Like the others in this class, she was self-conscious about writing in this complicated new language.

To break the ice for students like Sonia, I often start by asking the group how they slept last night, and if anyone remembers a dream. Soon the group is complaining about inadequate sleep or talking excitedly about their dreams. Then, I ask everyone to write down one dream they remember.

In Sonia's dream, a girl wearing a pink prom dress is trapped in the back seat of a car as it sinks into the depths of a lake. After reading over what she had written, I encouraged her to imagine various new endings for her dream. "Treat it like a story now," I told her, "something you might read in a book." Sonia liked this idea. She smiled and relaxed a bit as she described placing her hands on the steering wheel of that dream car and placing her foot on the gas.

I didn't get to know how Sonia's life turned out, but I like to think she might also have imagined where she might steer her own story, so as not to wind up at the bottom of some metaphoric lake, drowning in depression or despair. I can say, however, that by the end of that class, she exuded a new sense of calm and confidence.

I've seen other students face their fears of everything from snakes to speaking about childhood sexual abuse after participating in my workshops and classes. Blocked writers have found fluidity and fun on the page, and writers who couldn't access their dreams developed impressive recall.

One student came to her first Dreaming on the Page workshop saying she rarely remembered her dreams, but when she did they were repetitive and disturbing narratives about a camp cabin from her childhood. But after a four-week workshop, she developed an entirely new relationship with her dreams and writing. She said:

> In the past, I had thought that I mostly had bad dreams and night terrors. My dream recall worked much like the amygdala—recalling the big stuff out of context and letting the smaller things lay quieter. Seeing all my dreams side by side in my notebook reminds me that I have many dreams that have nothing to do with the cabin and even the ones that do go there can be mined for healing stones.

These experiences of the healing powers of dreamwork and writing are more than just a handful of anecdotes. Psychologist James W. Pennebaker's work on the salutary properties of writing have become widely accepted, and there are now graduate-level courses in expressive and therapeutic writing. As for dreams, starting with Freud and Jung, modern dreamwork has been used to accelerate healing in clinical settings, to help clients recover from trauma and grief, and to promote feelings of overall well-being. Renowned dreamworker Jeremy Taylor's adage that all dreams come in the service of health and wholeness is rooted in Jungian psychology that posits that the work of the subconscious mind is to help us achieve integration of all parts of ourselves, so we can fulfill our potential and live in harmony. As such, it's not surprising that writing and dreamwork together magnify the benefits from both therapeutic modalities. Dreaming on the Page helps us befriend all parts of ourselves and accelerate the work of integration and individuation—the gold standard for dreamwork and psychotherapy—so we can become healthy, whole, and happy. We look at the dream from different perspectives or we inhabit other skins as characters whose viewpoints, for a time, become our own. Both practices nurture awareness of a full range of emotional states and help soften our hearts.

Prompt: Something I Can't Forget

Even in our sleep, pain which cannot forget
falls drop by drop upon the heart . . .

—Aeschylus, ancient Greek tragedian

Use the Dreaming on the Page process to mine some healing stones. Reflect on the lines quoted above by the Greek poet Aeschylus (not to be confused with Asclepius, the god of medicine). Then, use one or more of these phrases to journal about dreams and healing:

Even in my sleep I can't forget _____
_____ *falls drop by drop upon my heart.*
Until, against my will comes _____

THE COLLECTIVE

> *The human kingdom, beneath the floor of the comparatively neat little dwelling that we call our consciousness, goes down into unsuspected Aladdin caves. There not only jewels but also dangerous jinn abide . . . that is the lure, the promise and terror of these disturbing night visitants from the mythological realm that we carry within us.*
>
> —Joseph Campbell, *The Hero with a Thousand Faces*

The Personal *Within* the Political

It was around the time that President John F. Kennedy was assassinated that I drew my wobbly infant self up to sit for the first time. I took my first steps in the twilight years of the civil rights struggle, and in elementary school, on my ten-year-old wrist, I wore a nickel-plated prisoner of war bracelet etched with the name of an American soldier who was missing somewhere in Vietnam. I learned long division just as the second wave of feminism was gathering steam, and when Ronald Reagan was elected president, during my senior year in high school, I had learned just enough about political science to piece together a dim understanding of why my mother thought his tenure in the White House spelled doom for American democracy. In college I first heard the slogan "The personal is political," and I took this sentiment to heart—or so I thought at the time.

But despite all that had been playing out on television and the front pages of the newspapers at the time, despite my studies of literature, history, and mythology, I still somehow believed that "all of that" was in the background—and I could create whatever life I pleased for myself. I had yet to fully absorb the fact that I was perched at the farthest tip of human experience to that point, and that beneath my feet was a pool of collective knowledge and cultural wisdom of unfathomable depths and a complex web of institutions that would determine my path as much as the choices I would make.

I don't think I'm alone in this. The insight that dreams guide our personal growth and psychological healing is among the great gifts that Sigmund Freud brought to contemporary dreamwork. But sadly, the rest of the message didn't stick: Dreams also guide and heal us as families, communities, countries, and even as a species. Understanding our individual lives in light of the collective is a big project. And although you or I might not be consciously aware of our place in the larger human story, our dreams are.

Jung popularized the idea of the collective unconscious and the role of dreams in helping us connect with this subterranean storehouse of group memory. But he didn't invent these ideas. In Indigenous cultures worldwide (some of which Jung studied as the basis for his theory of the collective unconscious), dreams are believed to carry messages for the community's well-being. The Iroquois of North America revered and routinely shared dreams and looked to dreams for guidance in tribal matters. In 1876, Sitting Bull was said to have foreseen the events of Little Bighorn in a vision or dream, which may have accounted for the Lakota Sioux victory over General Custer and his army. Also, in Tibetan dream yoga, working with dreams trains practitioners to prepare to navigate the bardo (realm between death and rebirth) so they can ultimately transcend the cycles of life, death, and reincarnation. According to legend, students of dream yoga were expected to gather in a classroom in lucid dreams, where they would be instructed by their dream teacher. An unexcused absence on the dream plane would be noted. Whether this description is actual or apocryphal, it exemplifies how dreams in some cultures are interwoven into people's spiritual education.

Whether we realize it or not, our dreams are calling us to take a wider view of the world and our place in it. When I was growing up among sidewalks, malls, and neatly measured lawns, my dreams opened avenues of possibility beyond the bounds of my suburban life. Yours are calling to you, too, inviting you into the collective stories unfolding all around.

Dateline REM

Imagine a world in which the pundits on the nightly news weigh in on big dreams from the day's breaking stories. What did the reigning monarch dream about last night? What recurring nightmare is plaguing the prime minister? Imagine the talking heads arguing over interpretations of what these dreams might mean and their implications for world capitals and warring nations. Even I, a professional dreamworker and former journalist, admit that's a far-fetched fantasy. After all, dreams rarely make the news at all, and when they do it's usually in the context of something that's been lost, as if dreams were a species that's quickly going extinct. Which isn't that far from the truth: The Centers for Disease Control and Prevention has deemed sleep loss an epidemic. Dream loss is a corollary to the widespread problem of sleep loss, and dreams are occasionally mentioned in this context.

Another time dreams make the news is in relationship to a new medication to induce sleep or cure nightmares, as when treatments for PTSD nightmares are discussed. Dreams also grab an occasional sensational headline during periods of paradigm-shaking crises, as after 9/11 when both dreams and poetry suddenly made the news, and again when pandemic dreams and poetry's importance claimed headlines in 2020 amid deadly surges in COVID-19 cases. Suddenly every media outlet from the *New York Times* to the *Huffington Post* was weighing in on the strange dreams that people seemed to be having during months of lockdown.

But just as quickly they vanish from public discourse.

Dreams as aspiration have a better chance of getting media attention. The #DREAMers hashtag went viral when undocumented students fought for their right to a college education and fair treatment. Dreams, used as a rhetorical device, woke us up to collective truths during the civil rights movement when Martin Luther King Jr. issued a clarion call for racial equality and justice that solemnized the words *I have a dream*. Climate activist Greta Thunberg spoke up for her generation in a fierce speech at the UN Summit in 2019. "You have stolen my dreams and my childhood with your empty words," she said.

Nonetheless, dreams are behind countless events that have shaped our world. Mahatma Gandhi claimed that a dream inspired him to lead the nonviolent protests that led to India's independence. Dreams were infamously behind the events of September 11, 2001, with members of al-Qaeda reporting that they dreamed of flying planes into towers in the weeks and months leading up to the attack on the World Trade Center. Who knows how many other events have been influenced by dreams. No one asks about them, so no one tells.

Still, these silent newsmakers persist. Even as they are denied airtime in private conversation and in political discussions, dreams continue to be an underground source of breaking news. Dreams, after all, offer an alternative form of thinking that everyone participates in, whether they get their news from Fox News, the BBC, the *People's Daily*, or MSNBC.

One day, perhaps, wisdom from the sleeping mind will break open a brighter consciousness that will help us fulfill our potential, both individually and globally. And maybe it will even be broadcast on the nightly news.

Investigate Your Dreams

Do some investigative reporting of your own to uncover how dreams have influenced your work, your relationships, and your sense of meaning or purpose. Use these questions to dig into the news stories from the night. Has a dream ever helped you with the following:

- A breakthrough (personally, creatively, and/or professionally)?
- A career change or redefining your purpose?
- Finding meaning or guidance in a time when you'd lost hope?
- Avoiding peril, such as with a warning about an illness or danger to you or a loved one?
- Imagining new approaches to a problem that you, your family, or community was facing?

Now consider these questions again, this time from the perspective of a character you are writing about.

Breaking S'news

As a reporter for a regional newspaper, I first covered rural hill towns, about which I joked there were more cows than people. Over the years I was assigned to larger beats including health, religion, higher education, and the arts. Perhaps that's why I sometimes think of the characters in my dreams as a team of reporters who are covering various beats within me: the health of my body, the state of my emotions, and bulletins from my soul's sanctuary, for example.

Sometimes I even write my dream reports as bulletins from the Land of Nod, and I ask my students to write theirs as news stories, too. Kat, a workshop participant who rewrote an epic dream in the form of a tabloid story, observed, "As a reporter I don't have to get into the emotions of it all. I can look at the dream objectively." Her piece was funny and engaging. Better yet, writing and reading it aloud to the group gave her a stroke of insight that other forms of dreamwork hadn't. "Now that I know that story, I choose to tell it differently," she said.

Pulling out our imaginary reporter's notebook and using dreams as fodder for reportage can help us identify the news that is breaking through from our subconscious mind. After all, our dreams, like skillful reporters, don't just tell us what we already know.

Prompt: J-School for Dreamers

Adopt a newshound's nose when perusing your dreams. Sniff out breaking stories, interesting details, informative sources, and quirky characters in the Land of Nod. What are the conflicts and issues facing the inhabitants of this region? What do you learn about your dreams from viewing them in this way?

You can experiment with different styles, too:

- Write a profile or Q&A-style interview with a dream character. Your finished product might read like something you'd see in your favorite lifestyle magazine.
- Or, report on a dream with the sobriety of a journalist who is tracking the ups and downs of the DOW and NASDAQ or the doings of world superpowers. Adopt a serious tone and stick to the facts.
- You can even try writing a dream in the style of your favorite gossip columnist or as if your dream is the Dear Abby of the Midnight Mind.

Whatever approach you take, try applying these newswriting conventions to your dream reports:

Lead with what's new. *Home invasions are on the rise in the Land of Nod, as an unprecedented number of suspicious characters have been found lurking outside of sleepers' homes.*

Include quotes. *"The doors won't lock properly," one exasperated homeowner reported. No matter how often she tried to dial 911 for help, "the phones just wouldn't work," she said.*

Voice-over. Imitate the voice of your favorite local news reporter, national or international correspondent, or news anchor. Have fun with this!

Be objective. Don't take sides; report the story from various angles, including from the perspective of the dream antagonist and innocent bystanders.

Headliners. Headlines are similar to dream titles, but a headline has the special job of hooking the reader's attention with what's new and noteworthy. Try giving your dreams headlines: *"Long-Lost Niece Makes Surprise Appearance at Birthday Party"* or *"Bridge Jumper's Desperate Plunge Interrupted by Passing Stranger"* or *"Suburban Housewife Courted by Presidential Hopeful,"* etc. Notice how giving a dream a headline, rather than a more workaday or literary title, changes the sense of urgency or meaning in the dream.

Dreams in Review

Review your dreams to see what personal—and collective—issues they are reporting on. Ask some or all of the following questions. Take your time—there's no deadline to meet:

1. What new story about a recurring situation in my life have my dreams been trying to tell me?
2. How can I use the stories my dreams are telling me to help me imagine a more promising future for my community or the world at large? (Look for references to larger world events tucked into your dreams to find hints.)
3. What other realms beyond my day-to-day activities might my dreams be informing me about: Spiritual? Health? Ecological? What else?

> *As you enter positions of trust and power,*
> *dream a little before you think.*
>
> —Toni Morrison, novelist

The Healer at the Edge of the Village

There's a traditional story (which I've adapted) about a village that was experiencing a severe drought. The earth was parched, crops were dying, and people's hopes were beginning to wither along with the grasses and trees. The townspeople sent for a healer who was said to work miracles, which was just what they needed.

When the healer finally arrived, the people asked her what they should do. She said, "Build me a hut at the farthest edge of the village, away from everyone." The townspeople did what was asked. Then the healer retreated into the solitude of the newly built hut, and she wasn't seen or heard from for several days.

Just as the villagers began to lose hope, rain began to fall! The precipitation was welcomed and they collected plenty of water for their needs.

The healer at last emerged and was greeted with cheers of gratitude, followed by questions about what she did to bring the rain.

She replied, "I saw that things were out of balance here, so I went inside until I could bring myself into harmony. There can be no balance on the outside until there is harmony on the inside."

I think of this story when I take in the news and witness what is happening in the world: pandemic, war, uprisings, oil spills, cataclysmic weather events, fires, injustice. Sometimes I wish for a leader who can put the world right. In the meantime, I compose letters to elected officials and mail postcards to encourage people to register to vote. But I realize that not all help comes from the outside. Each of us must find balance and harmony within, too.

Elizabeth Lesser, author of *Cassandra Speaks,* coined the word *innervism* as the necessary counterpoint to activism. She writes, "If we focus only on fighting what we perceive to be wrong *out there*, we miss out on the very real work waiting to be done within our own hearts and minds and lives."

As a conscious dreamer, I know that what I see outside is a projection of what lies inside. It's easy to say I'm for peace because I don't have the power or inclination to wage war against nations. But I often wage war within my own heart and mind. I grow impatient with what is, I rail against opinions I disagree with, I hold silent grudges, and I judge people more often than I would like. Once, at a rally for peace and justice, I found myself shouting at counterprotesters who were shouting at me. We were mirror images of red-faced rage. It felt good at first to vent my anger, but I knew better and quickly walked away.

Until we do the work to make inner peace, we project our conflicts beyond the boundaries of our own skin. Ours may be small transgressions compared to corporate greed, political malfeasance, and actual warfare, but large systems are made up of individuals. And we carry our rucksacks laden with toxic thoughts wherever we go.

While participating in our own inner work, or innervism, is not enough, activism without innervism can be counterproductive. Writing and dreamwork are forms of inner work that help us activate healthier relationships with ourselves, with our close circle of family, friends, colleagues, and community. These practices can make us more thoughtful, responsive (instead of reactive) activists as well.

When writing in our journals, we can pause at each implicit or explicit belief we express and ask ourselves: What evidence do I have for this belief? Are my sources trustworthy? Is this belief outdated? Does it still hold up? Is it time to revise it?

Then we can take our writing to the next level: We can write a letter to the editor or to our local representatives, publish a poem, or read aloud to a group of friends or strangers to move our personal writing to the wider world.

We can also use our dreamwork skills to approach the news of local, national, and international events as collective or mutual dreams. Then we can explore them the same way we'd work on a nightmare. In what ways might the characters and scenarios represent a repressed or rejected part of ourselves? Once we see the pattern or problem inside us, we can begin to take steps to address its manifestations in the outer world with more empathy and compassion.

When we work from the inside out, we are better equipped to step into the world and affirm and protect our highest values. The interior work that we engage in through writing and dreamwork contributes to our collective healing in ways beyond what we can imagine.

No one has seen the night sky from exactly your trajectory. No one has loved exactly the people and places that you have loved. Who will tell that part of the earth's story, if you do not?

—Pat Schneider, *Writing Alone and with Others*

Dreaming Forward

If we want to see more goodness in the world, we have to get interested in goodness. We must tell good stories and use our literary gifts and dreamwork to manifest our hopes and wishes for a more just and joyful world.

You don't have to write polemics to contribute to social justice through writing. Like writers across genres, including poetry (Naomi Shihab Nye or Dwayne Betts), science fiction (Octavia Butler), or romance novels (Stacey Abrams aka Selena Montgomery), and countless others, you can incorporate an awareness of social justice into whatever you are writing. Even simple but profound acts like using inclusive pronouns or becoming conscious of the racial assumptions that are built into your work can make a world of difference.

What change will you make through your Dreaming on the Page practice to help you dream up a world filled with integrity, virtue, love, dazzle, and fun?

CIRCLES OF
CONNECTION

I have spread my dreams under your feet;
Tread softly because you tread on my dreams.

—William Butler Yeats,
"He Wishes for the Cloths of Heaven"

Dream and Write Together

These days, the closest approximation most of us have to the sacred, ancient experience of dream sharing or storytelling is in dream circles and writing groups. Unlike telling dreams to our therapist, or hearing stories at literary readings on college campuses or at bookstores (wonderful as those are), these groups and circles are places where we have a communal, noncommercial, egalitarian, and authentic experience of sharing dreams and stories.

In Dreaming on the Page workshops, we share both dreams and literary creations. I encourage you to join a DOTP workshop, or create a DOTP circle of your own. If you do, you can use the exercises and prompts in this book as a guide. What follows are some points to keep in mind when creating your DOTP circle.

Getting Started

The guidelines in this section help create a safe and welcoming environment—and a productive one—for DOTP circles:

Form a group of any size. When it comes to the size of your group, look for that Goldilocks sweet spot. Working in a pair with a close friend is just the right fit for some. But if you want to form a group, I suggest a circle of three to six members. More than that can get unwieldy and can make it difficult for each member to have time to write and share their work.

Make a meeting place. The composition of your group might determine where you will meet. Members who live close to one another can meet at one another's homes, or if your posse lives far apart, meeting online is a great way to bring your group together. Closeness and community can be achieved either way.

Set a schedule. Decide how often you'd like your group to meet and for how long. Once or twice a month is usually a good fit and allows members time to collect new dreams in between meetings. Sessions of ninety minutes and up to two hours tend to be ideal to maintain the group's focus and also allow sufficient time for the group's activities.

Decide on a commitment. It can take some time for a group to hit its stride and to get a feel for what's working and what's not. Agree to meet for six sessions to start with. After that you can assess how your group is working out, and whether you want to fine-tune your meeting structure or process. Then, recommit to another six weeks—or longer—as your group sees fit.

Follow the leader. It's important to have a facilitator who will open the circle, offer a prompt, and keep time. Decide ahead of time whether you will have one facilitator for all of your meetings, or if you want to rotate leadership responsibilities.

Keep time. There never seems to be enough time for dream-work or sharing writing. By the same token, it's amazing what can happen in even a brief amount of time when we keep our focus. Starting and ending groups on time, and setting time limits for each activity within the group, helps build a safe and reliable container for group work.

Group Structure

As in writing, structure gives form to the group while opening space for creative expression. Follow this basic outline, along with the rest of the guidelines in this section, for your DOTP circle:

1. **Check-in.** Each session should start with a brief check-in from each member, consisting of a word or phrase to describe how they are feeling, and a dream title. (This can be the title of a dream they plan to work on or not. Any dream title will do.)

2. **Get centered**. To help each member begin to turn inward, and to touch in with their body, breath, and emotions, offer a few moments of silence, or a two- to three-minute guided meditation.
3. **Time to write**. A prompt should be offered, followed by time to write. Each group session might consist of one short write (four to seven minutes of writing) and one longer one (twenty to forty minutes), depending on the number of members and the available time. Either way, use any of the prompts in this book to help inspire members to get started.
4. **Time to share**. After each writing session, participants are encouraged to read their work aloud and receive strength-based feedback. See the guidelines in this section for more details.
5. **Closing time**. Close the circle with another brief meditation to allow the benefits of the session to sink in.

Safety in Sharing

To make your DOTP circle a welcoming space, agree to a set of guidelines to ensure confidentiality and to affirm the dreamy writer's authority over their dreams and stories. Here are the Dreaming on the Page guidelines for safety in sharing, which I recommend. Print them out and make a copy for each participant. Be sure that each member commits to abide by each statement during your first group meeting, and review them at regular intervals to keep the group healthy:

> **The Vegas rule.** We observe strict confidentiality in our groups. What's said in a DOTP circle stays in our circle.
> **Prompt or not.** Writing in response to the prompts provided by the facilitator can shake you out of old habits and inspire you to explore new territory. That said, participants can modify the prompt—or even skip it—to suit their needs and writing goals.
> **Speaking of dreams.** In DOTP circles we affirm that the dreamer is the authority on the meaning of their own dream.

Other members are invited to listen to the dream as if it were their own and discover what it means for *them*, using the phrase "As my dream" to introduce their comments about it. This way we never hijack someone else's dream, and we each gain the benefit of discovering the dream's message for ourselves.

Receive, receive. When someone shares a dream or piece of writing with the group, we practice active listening and receive what is said (and read) with open, patient, curious, nonjudgmental, and loving attention.

Look for the good. When we offer feedback, we respect the fact that both dreams and creative writing carry a lot of emotion and can bring up feelings of vulnerability. We offer gentle, strength-based responses to what we hear. We might comment on what we like in a piece of writing, what stays with us, what surprises us, and what intrigues us.

Works of fiction. We regard all writing as works of fiction, whether or not we think we recognize a story as the writer's own experience. We don't assume that the narrator in a piece of writing is the same as the author. This is an important shift in perspective that allows participants the safety and freedom to write whatever is in their hearts.

A shared birthright. Dreams and storytelling are inherent to all people all over the world, to people of all language groups and all ethnic, racial, and religious groups. They come equally to people no matter what their economic or educational background. We welcome, honor, and deeply respect everyone in our groups. We come together for our shared interest in dreams, writing, and creativity and not to debate, convince, or correct anyone on their belief systems that may differ from our own.

Take care. Take good care of yourself in the group; let the group leader know if you need something so they can support you in getting it.

While we can never guarantee emotional safety, adhering to these guidelines can help us create the conditions for a supportive experience when sharing dreams and writing.

What was your dream?

I long to hear you tell it.

—Shakespeare, *Richard III*

Listen Carefully

Reading aloud in Dreaming on the Page circles is not a performance, nor is it a request for approval. Our purpose is to hear our writing aloud. When we listen to one another read, we maintain an attitude of curiosity that is free of judgment, evaluation, or critique. We don't tell the writer how to improve or fix their writing. Nor is it our job to bestow or withdraw approval. Instead, we share what images stayed with us, what the writing made us think about, and what surprised us.

The process goes like this:

1. Each writer takes a turn reading their work aloud as if they found this piece of writing in their favorite bookstore inside a volume by a beloved author. In other words, she reads with the expectation of falling in love with this piece of writing.
2. Group members listen to what they are hearing as if they themselves wrote it. This shifts the listener into the first-person position. Listening in this way helps us experience the work rather than evaluating it or judging it.
3. Similar to a noninterpretive approach to dreamwork, when we respond to writing in DOTP circles, we don't analyze it or try to change what we are hearing. We offer

observations, not directives. These prompts help keep the focus on our experience of the work rather than a critique of it:

Listening to this piece, I feel . . .
These phrases, images, or specific moments in the piece stood out for me . . .
because . . .
What I love about this piece is . . . [be specific]
This piece prompted this insight for me . . .

4. When the group is finished responding, the writer has the last word. She shares her own observations of writing and hearing her work, as well as any insights that might have arisen from the group members' responses.

Group Play

Creating a Dreaming on the Page circle allows you to nurture and explore the collective aspects of working with dreams and the imagination. Groups can also be a lot of fun. You can use any of the exercises in this book as prompts for the group. In addition, the following prompt takes the collective nature of writing a step further, by creating a collaborative work.

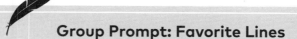

Group Prompt: Favorite Lines

1. At the end of a group session, the facilitator asks each member to write their favorite line from the day's writing onto a slip of paper (or if meeting online, they can write their line in the chat panel).
2. The facilitator (or a volunteer from the group) collects the favorite lines, then reads them aloud in the order that they appear in the pile of slips of paper, or in the chat panel.
3. It is optional to have a group member act as the scribe, writing the lines in order on a sheet of paper so the group poem can be photocopied or typed up and distributed at the next meeting.
4. The result will be a surrealistic—but often meaningful and/ or comical—and surprisingly complete poem.

ACKNOWLEDGMENTS

A book, like a dream, is a co-creation. Here some of the people who helped me to create this one:

Thank you to the creative team at the Collective Book Studio, especially Angela Engel, Ruby Privateer, Dean Burrell, and Elisabeth Saake, who helped shape this dream into the book you are now reading.

I would also like to express gratitude to my family of dreamers who are part of the International Association for the Study of Dreams—especially my mentor and colleague Justina Lasley.

A book is a dream that you hold in your hand.

—Neil Gaiman, novelist

I am deeply grateful to the writers in my life who read and commented on drafts of this book, including my Writing Roomies at Forbes Library; The Backroom Writers: Charlotte Meryman, Sean Norton, and Rachel Hass; and big, blossoming bouquets of gratitude to Grace Welker, Elise Gibson, and Sherry Puricelli who read drafts of this book and cheered me on. For long and uplifting talks about writing, publishing, editing, and everything else, I thank Karen Levy, Lori Soderlind, and Lesléa Newman. A special thank-you goes to Patricia Lee Lewis and Linda Trichter Metcalf, who have helped shape my ideas about writing and teaching.

Thank you to all of my students and clients, from whom I learn so much. A special shout-out goes to Beth Ann Jedziniak for first suggesting that I put what we do together in Dreaming on the Page workshops into a book.

Thank you to Aja Riggs, for being there through everything, and for a very long time. And I offer a heart full of gratitude to my loving and supportive family, especially Miranda Sanders, Richard and Diane Gover, James Gover, and my late mother, Jane Covell (who continues to visit my dreams). I am grateful beyond words, every day, for my husband, Louis Moore.

An anonymous stranger placed a goal-setting journal in a Little Free Library box in my neighborhood with a sticky note that read: "Intended for hitting a serious goal in 100 days." I took that book, and the challenge, to write the first draft of this book. Thank you, stranger!

And, of course, I owe unending thanks to my dreams for a lifetime of generous guidance and inspiration.

APPENDIX

The Four Basic Skills for Dreaming on the Page

Anyone can benefit from the Dreaming on the Page approach to writing, whether you remember dreams or not. But these four basic skills can help you be a more active and engaged dreamer, and refining them will open new possibilities for your creative work as well. What follows is a brief introduction to each one.

Dream Recall

To increase dream recall, keep a notebook and pencil by your bed to write your dreams, and try the following:

Write it out. Write out your intention to recall your dreams in your notebook before you go to sleep. In the morning write something down—a dream, dream snippet, or fragment. If you don't remember a dream at first, write the words *Last night I dreamed . . .* and wait a moment, and see what comes. If no dreams come to mind, write down *something* about your experience of the night (for example: *Last night I slept soundly*, or *Last night I lay awake listening to my dog snore*, etc.).

Wake naturally. It's ideal to wake without an alarm clock. That's because your last REM period, the one you have just before waking in the morning, is the longest and usually filled with vivid narrative dreams. The sudden intrusion of the alarm can wake you before the dream begins or it can truncate the dream. Unfortunately, most of us can't afford to risk waking without an alarm, but you can do this: Set your alarm for fifteen minutes after your ideal wake-up time to give yourself a chance to wake naturally—or consider investing in an alarm clock that wakes you slowly with gradually increasing light. If all else fails, wake naturally on your days off to reap a healthy dream harvest.

Be still. Some mornings, catching dreams feels like trying to catch fish bare-handed—they slip away before you can manage to hold on. Lie still in bed before you open your eyes and try to recall your dreams before your daytime mind kicks in. Or, if you've already started to rouse, return to the same position you slept in, and remain there for a few breaths. Often this helps bring the dream memories back.

Beyond words. Because imagery is the dream's primary language, sometimes drawing rather than writing the dreams is a good practice. Experiment to see if this helps bring back more of the dream.

Roll call. If you wake up with no dream recall, think of the people and situations you often dream about, and one by one, call each to mind. For example, ask yourself: Did I dream about my mother? Did I dream about houses? Any chase scenes? Pause between each question. A dream might come to mind. Just reaching back toward your dreams can sometimes prompt a memory of one.

After a week or two of committing to this practice, you'll likely be recalling dreams with greater ease.

Dream Incubation Basics

While we tend to think dreams are purely random occurrences over which we have no control, the practical reality is quite different. With even a little effort and practice, most anyone can learn to incubate a dream. The instructions are quite simple:

- Practice remembering your dreams using the suggestions above.
- Before bed, set an intention for what issue you want to dream about. For example, *Tonight I'll see what is blocking me from making progress in my writing.* Or, *Tonight I'll see what my next book will be about.* Or, *Show me what I need to know in my life right now.* Pose open-ended questions (yes/no questions are not effective) and use wording that asks to see or be shown something whenever possible, because dreams speak primarily in a visual language.
- Put a picture or object that represents your intention (for a question about writing, it might be a book, an image that

represents a character in a story you are writing, or even a special pen) near your bed, or under your pillow or mattress. Doing so helps solidify your intention.

- Repeat your intention one to three times in your mind as you are falling asleep, and then again if you wake in the middle of the night.
- Record your dream in the morning and review it for any ways it might connect with your intention. If you don't recall any dreams, write something in your notebook anyway, such as *"I woke up feeling..."* Or *"I woke up thinking about..."* That will prime your dream recall for next time. It may take several tries before you catch a dream. Be patient.

Incubating dreams is a great way to receive guidance and practice looking inward for answers. It is also a way to practice focusing your thoughts and attention—skills that are helpful in all aspects of your life, including writing.

Dream Lucidity Basics

It sounds crazy at first: You know that you're dreaming while you're dreaming, so rather than just being swept up in the action of the dream, you can make choices and do what you want. For instance, you can hop a train in Duluth and travel directly to the Alps in the space of one breath. You might even do backflips even though in waking reality you can't even do a somersault.

Put simply, lucid dreaming is a hybrid state of consciousness in which you simultaneously enjoy the creative brain chemistry of dreaming *and* facets of your daytime logical thinking. There are many resources to help you learn to have lucid dreams. Here are a few tips to help you get started:

1. **Begin by day**. During the day, stop several times at random (you can set an alert on your watch or phone to remind you) and ask, *Am I awake or dreaming?* Pause before you answer and consider the question. What evidence do you have that you are truly awake?

2. **Perform a state check**. Normally, it's easy to say that we are awake when we're up and about during the day. But in dreams it's not as easy. We are swept up in the dream, unaware that our body is asleep in bed. So, practice answering this seemingly simple question while you're awake. When you ask, *Am I awake or dreaming?*, do a state check before answering the question. An easy one is to check the time. Look at a clock, your watch, or phone and note the time. Look away for a few seconds, then look back. If you are awake, the time will be the same, or close to it. Asleep, when you look at your watch, the time may be a scramble of numbers. Or, when you check back after a moment, the time may have jumped ahead to 37 o'clock, or your watch may have disappeared altogether. Then you know you are dreaming.

3. **Be prepared**. After a few nights, or perhaps a week or two of trying, many people achieve dream lucidity. When that happens, have a question prepared. You can use your dream incubation question, or use an all-purpose request such as, *Show me what I need to see right now*. You can also decide to fly, which is a fun and liberating dream experience.

4. **Try again**. If you don't get lucid right away—or at all— don't be discouraged. Practice lucidity any time you're awake. Ask yourself, *Am I truly awake in this moment?* Pause and consider the answer. Are you awake to the wonder of being alive? Are you fully present with what is? If not, keep practicing waking up to the precious gift of the present moment. After all, the goal of all dreamwork, writing, and dream lucidity is to wake up to the wonders of the world around us.

Active and Engaged Listening

Just as with dreaming, we often mistakenly consider listening to be a passive activity. In Dreaming on the Page, we regard listening as a skill that can be practiced and improved to enhance our experiences of dreams, writing, and wide-awake living. You will find descriptions of active and engaged listening throughout this book. Here is a summary of the key components:

Patient. Listen like you have nowhere else to be. Listen for what will come next, listen to the silences between words, listen without trying to control what you are hearing.

Curious. Lean in and listen. Why does the writer/speaker believe what they believe? What evidence do they have for their point of view? Get curious about your reactions to what you're hearing, too.

Nonjudgmental. Maintain a state of open receptivity as you listen. When you notice that you're judging what you hear, reset your intention. Be patient with yourself: Simply noticing that you're judging is the first step to becoming a nonjudgmental listener.

Loving. When we listen to someone with patient, curious, nonjudgmental attention, it is, in effect, an act of love. To bring even more love to the conversation—with yourself, your dreams, your writing, and others—try moving your attention from your head to your heart as you listen.

Endnotes

1. Roberta Binkley, "Biography of Enheduanna, Priestess of Inanna" Feminist Theory Website, 1998, http://www.cddc.vt.edu/feminism/Enheduanna.html.

2. Alice Robb, *Why We Dream* (Boston: Mariner Books, 2019), p. 14.

3. Michael Chabon in an interview by Killian Fox, Sept. 9, 2012, https://www.theguardian.com/books/2012/sep/09/michael-chabon-telegraph-avenue-interview.

4. Ross Gay described his process in an interview with Ari Shapiro on National Public Radio, "Encore: Ross Gay Writes 'The Book of Delights,'" *All Things Considered*, March 23, 2020.

5. Matthew Zapruder, "Whirl," *New York Times,* Sunday Magazine, May 28, 2017, p. 19.

6. According to Alice W. Flaherty, writing in *The Midnight Disease* (New York: Houghton Mifflin Harcort, 2004, p. 96), Freud may have gotten the idea for free association from an 1823 essay by Ludwig Börne, "The Art of Becoming an Original Writer in Three Days."

7. Tzivia Gover, "Our Return to Tenderness," *The New York Times,* September 17, 2019, Styles, p. 6.

8. This exercise, based on a technique used in Gestalt therapy, has been adapted from Robert Hoss in *Dream Language* (Ashland, OR: Innersource, 2005).

9. It is interesting to note that Catherine Gilbert Murdock has said that her dreams have sparked her fiction.

For bonus material including resources and a list of works cited, use this QR code or visit: www.dreamingonthepage.com/more.